BELIEF ALCHEMIST

Change your beliefs, transform your life!

MARIA J MCMAHON

Published by Still Pool Publishing

Illustrations by Ruth Arbon
Formatting and Interior Design by Woven Red Author Services

ISBN ebook: 978-1-7398493-1-3
ISBN 6" x 9"print book: 978-1-7398493-0-6
ISBN 5" x 8" print book: 978-1-7398493-2-0

Disclaimer

The results obtained from using the Belief Alchemist book, exercises and techniques will vary depending on individual differences, such as willingness to heal and the amount of time and effort dedicated towards achieving that, along with many other variables. Maria J McMahon does not assume responsibility for results obtained from using the Belief Alchemist book, exercises or techniques. Belief Alchemist does not claim to diagnose, treat, or heal any existing medical conditions or to act as a substitute for medical advice or treatment for any physical or mental health conditions. Anyone who is currently receiving treatment from their doctor, or any other trained medical professional should continue with their treatment. Due to the deep introspective nature of the Belief Alchemist exercises and techniques, it is possible that you may uncover painful memories or issues from the past. Belief Alchemist is a self-help book and therefore the use of the book including the exercises and techniques are undertaken at your own risk. Maria J McMahon cannot be held liable for any possible ramifications of using the exercise or techniques included in Belief Alchemist including but not limited to depression, anxiety, suicidal thoughts or any other response to the Belief Alchemist book, techniques or exercises. Maria J McMahon is not liable for any damages of any kind arising out of the use of the Belief Alchemist book, exercises or techniques. By using this book in any form, you agree to the above terms.

Caution: Do not listen to the audio version of Belief Alchemist whilst driving or operating machinery.

Dedicated to my kind and courageous children Rhi and Ben.
I couldn't be more proud of you.

Also thank you to Ruth Arbon for producing
such brilliant illustrations.

Contents

Alchemist: ‘A person who transforms or creates something through a process that appears to be magical’.

Alchemy Four

For all of the children raised in the dark who manage to find their way back to their hearts;

A braver soldier has never been seen than the little boy of four years old, with no one to love him, and no one to hold. With fear in his heart that he'll never be seen, and reason to wonder the point of his being.

So he decides to go and live in his head and dream of better worlds instead, but after a while he loses himself, and begins to imagine he's somebody else.

Detached from his heart, he feels numb, but safe, from the terrible 'truths' he cannot yet face. So he builds an acceptable face for the world, whilst behind the mask the little boy lays, curled up and sobbing alone in the caves...

When the man's grown up, he decides to be brave and look for the little boy lost in the caves. Knowing now it's time to start the difficult road back to his heart.

He takes his time and spends the days, moving through caves of repression and rage. Layer by layer he moves slowly through, until he discovers the ultimate truth. The truth that the little boy never was told, as he sobbed in his bed, at four years old.

That his parents were children raised in the dark who never found their way back to their hearts. So they passed on to him their anger and fear, and feeling not good enough to be here, and with that the lie (that feels like a curse) that we live in an unfriendly universe

As the boy listened carefully to what he was told, his tight little body began to unfold, and a smile bright as day shone from his face, as he now understood divinity's grace...

That we're all bound together by a force from above, the force of unconditional love. It runs straight through the core of our being, it's only the lie that stops us from seeing. That we're worthy and loved, despite the times we've felt estranged from the Divine.

So here's how a man moved past the curse and found the friendly universe.

And now he cheers on those who start, to find their own way back to their hearts...

M J McMahon

Introduction

Hello and welcome, fellow Alchemist!

I'm so happy you found your way here and that I'm able to share with you some of the things that helped me along my journey to finding self-acceptance, self-love, and a deeper understanding of the truth of who I am.

We are all unique and beautiful expressions of the creative intelligence I call The Divine. For those of you who have had negative experiences of religion, I get it, I'm not religious myself; however, as a result of many personal experiences, I believe in what people call by various different names including God, The Divine, or Infinite Intelligence, to name just a few. If you don't share my belief that's totally okay, but please don't allow the words I use to describe the incredible creative system that lives inside each one of us to stop you from benefitting from the user manual for your mind laid down in this book.

We are all powerful creators of our own reality whether we are conscious of this, or not. That which is within us, our inner world, is constantly being expressed in our outer world. You will have experienced flashes of this truth throughout your life, and most likely passed them off as coincidence, whilst a deeper part of you is left wondering 'what if there's something more to this...?'

Deep-seated beliefs of unworthiness that got wired in during childhood, coupled with the fact that we are educated **out** of our ability to understand, and work with the creative system that is our mind, have left most people in ignorance of who they really are, and of what they are truly capable of. Anybody who is struggling with a lack of confidence and self-worth will be carrying **mistaken beliefs of unworthiness** that are getting in the way of them finding their purpose and creating a life they love.

You may not be fully aware of this, because on a conscious level you probably have *some* idea of your own worth; however, on an unconscious level **we all** carry limiting beliefs running in the background of our mind and getting in our way.

This results in a constant battle between your conscious sense of self-worth and your subconscious beliefs of unworthiness. This battle is often experienced as feeling 'blocked', or through behaviours like procrastination, or self-sabotage. Almost anything that stands in the way of your creating the life you want can be attributed to limiting beliefs. Carrying limiting beliefs is not only exhausting and frustrating; it also keeps you from **aligning your mind** in such a way as to achieve all that is possible in your life.

There's a reason why we're all born different. We each come into this life with something special to do here on earth. We are gifted and talented in different ways. This is encoded into our DNA and is unique to each one of us. As unique as your finger print. It is only through a lack of knowledge and understanding of the way we operate, that we are kept from discovering and fulfilling our Life's purpose.

I wrote Belief Alchemist with a view to helping you to hack into the belief cave inside your own subconscious mind, and to clear out any old limiting beliefs you carry, so that you are able to see yourself more clearly, as the Divine sees you. After clearing out the false beliefs stored in your subconscious, you will be able to align your mind in such a way as to draw to yourself health, wealth, love and the perfect expression of your soul here on earth. In other words, I wrote this book to teach you how to become your own Belief Alchemist, to step into your authentic power and create the life you want.

Before getting into the process of clearing limiting beliefs, I want to spend some time talking about the different aspects of your mind and how to access them, so that you can recognise the different states of mind easily, and become more aware of which state of mind you're in at any given time.

PART 1

'Who looks outside, dreams; who looks inside awakes'
~ CG Jung[1]

[1] C.G. Jung Letters Vol. 1: 1906-1950, page33

Welcome to your Mind

As human beings we are not naturally fixed in any one area of our mind, but instead move in and out of different areas (or states of consciousness) all the time. We were made this way for several reasons, one of them being that we are all natural creators and the different states of consciousness are there to assist us in this process in their own unique ways.

We are not taught how to utilise our creative power at school and our modern technology, if not used in a mindful and self-disciplined way, keeps us from accessing the different states of consciousness necessary to create a life we love, whilst also causing anxiety through keeping us stuck in our thinking mind for unnaturally long periods, and at the same time programming our subconscious mind with beliefs and images we don't want.

Only when we realise the truth of this can we become empowered as creators of our own life. Our first job is to clear out any limiting beliefs hiding away in our subconscious. This does not need to be our *exclusive* focus, however, as you will find that as you begin to take charge of your mind in the way explained in this book and start taking action towards your goals, the limiting beliefs hidden from you in your subconscious will make themselves known to you and this awareness will allow you to challenge and change them using the techniques in Part 2 of this book.

In the following pages I'm going to explain the different aspects of your mind. My explanations are not 'scientific' as I'm not a scientist, and there is still very much that science has yet to understand about the way our minds operate. My aim throughout this book is to increase your awareness of how your mind works, so to make things as clear as possible I have personified the different aspects of the mind to make them more identifiable. In this section I have also added different ways in which you can connect with the different areas of your mind.

We each possess four aspects to our minds:

1. Consciousness (Your Observer Self)
2. The Divine or Superconscious mind (Your Creator Self)
3. The Subconscious mind (Your Genie)
4. The Conscious, or Thinking mind (Your personal Secretary/Bodyguard)

Understanding how to get these different aspects of your mind to work together, **aligned in purpose** is the key to navigating life in a positive way, and creating the life you want.

Your Consciousness (Your Observer Self)

Another word to describe your consciousness is to call it your awareness. It is ever present whatever state of mind you're in, as a silent observer although ironically, you may not always be aware of it. Certain states of mind, like fear or anxiety, can result in a loss of conscious connection to our awareness for a while. With practice we can learn how to move out of fear states of mind quite quickly and into more peaceful states. The more we understand about how our mind works, and practice using it in a way that serves us, the better we become at being able to access different states of mind at will. Your consciousness is powerful. Not only does it affect your life, but it also affects whatever you place it on. Our consciousness energises whatever we place it on, so it's important that we place it on what we want to empower and create, and withdraw it from anything we do not want to empower. Think of your consciousness as being the ever-present silent overseer of your mind.

The Divine Mind (Your Creator Self)

Your Divine mind is your Creator Self. It knows your life's purpose and what will make you happy. It communicates with you through ideas, inspirations, intuitive insights, and solutions. These inspirations come to you in flashes throughout your life. You may be walking in the park one day and suddenly an idea flashes across your mind; you see yourself dancing in the sunshine in a foreign country, and think 'Wow! I would love to do that!' Or you may be talking to a friend when you suddenly have a moment of clarity on a problem you've been trying to solve. We all have flashes of inspiration like this, they come through to us like magical falling stars. This is your Divine Creator mind speaking to you. **So pay attention**. Grab hold of these flashes of inspiration and don't allow your thinking mind, or another person to talk you out of them. Hold the inspiring pictures and thoughts in your mind as you move throughout your day. Meditate on them often, allowing all of the blissful details of the life you want to create to emerge through to you from your Creator self. This is **why we possess an imagination**! It's a manifestation tool. Make this focus on the life you want to create a daily practice, feeling just as grateful for it **in the present** as you expect to feel when it becomes your reality.

To get scientific about it, use your imagination to create the same emotional frequency you expect to emit when you are living the life of your dreams. This will cause you to draw to yourself all that is a match to that frequency, and your subconscious mind will get to work on making your dreams a reality.

Gratitude is a Creative State of Consciousness!

The subject of gratitude comes up frequently when discussing manifestation and for very good reason! Acquiring and retaining a state of gratitude keeps you connected with the genius of your Divine Creator mind like nothing else. This is because gratitude is a creative state of consciousness.

So, developing a gratitude practice is **essential** if you are to become all that you are capable of becoming. A good way to develop and grow your gratitude muscle is to exercise it as much as possible. Make a habit of practicing gratitude as soon as you wake up, before you fall asleep, and lots of times in between. Keeping a gratitude journal is a good way to stay consistent and also, getting into the habit of appreciating the everyday things in life, like healthy food and fresh air. It is for this reason that I have created a Gratitude journal to use alongside this book.

The more you practice gratitude, the closer your connection to your Divine Creator mind becomes, and the easier it is to receive creative ideas and guidance on how to manifest them. Think of Gratitude as your Wi-Fi connection to your Divine Creator mind and keep it switched on!

The Subconscious Mind (Your Genie)

The subconscious mind is like an impartial faithful servant who waits for instructions on what it is you would like to create in your life. It is a **constant observer** that **hangs on your every word**, taking very seriously what you say to and about yourself and the world, and working (even during sleep) to bring your words into reality. It is for this reason that it's very important to pay *careful attention* to your words, and also to what you feed your subconscious mind through being mindful of **what you focus on**. If you are not feeding your subconscious mind **yourself** *deliberately* and *consciously*, through being mindful of what you read, watch, talk about etc... it will be taking in whatever random things you ***are*** focusing on and bringing more of ***that*** into your reality. So be sure to step into the position of being the boss of your own subconscious mind, or someone else will be using ***your*** servant to manifest ***their*** reality.

A good way to look at this (as you will see later) is to view your subconscious mind as being your own personal Genie. Be sure that **you** are the one giving your Genie the instructions. This is simply a matter of having the discipline to keep your mind **focused on what you want to create**, and that is where the thinking mind comes in.

The Thinking Mind (Your Personal Secretary/ Bodyguard)

The thinking mind is your will power, rationale, organiser and bodyguard. It gets things done. It directs your **focus** and action steps. What we focus on we empower, so it's extremely important to place your focus on what you want to create and to *keep it there* as much as possible. The job of your thinking mind is to act as Personal Secretary to your Divine Creator mind, working to keep you focused on bringing the creative inspirations received from your Creator mind into reality through taking practical action steps, whilst also acting as your personal bodyguard, keeping you safe, well and grounded in the world.

In Western society, we have been schooled into placing our thinking mind in chief position, as The CEO of our mind, and to pretty much ignore our Superconscious and Subconscious minds, as if they didn't exist. The problem with this is that it leaves us out of touch with our deepest desires and with the creative impulses of our Divine Creator mind that convey to us our life's purpose. It also keeps us from using our powerful Genie (subconscious mind) to manifest **our life's purpose**.

Not being in touch with what we want for *ourselves* leaves us open to also having our Personal Secretary/Bodyguard used to create someone else's reality and to never finding fulfilment in **our own life**. It also leaves us open to having the bodyguard aspect of our mind hijacked by **fear**! The bodyguard aspect of our thinking mind is always scanning for danger because it's there to protect us, so if it's not being used in a balanced way, aligned with the rest of our mind with the purpose of fulfilling our goals, it tends to go rogue and either make up its own scary stories, or to cling to scary stories you hear from friends, or see in the media. The problem with this is that not only is it distracting, but because our bodies don't know the difference between truth and reality and readily accept whatever it is we focus on as being true, focusing on fear creates uncomfortable fear states within our body that can be difficult to shake off.

So it's very important that we organise our mind to run the way it was designed to, with our **Divine Creator mind** as The CEO, **The Subconscious mind** (our Genie) working day and night on manifesting the desires and inspirations of our Divine Creator mind, and our **Thinking Mind** (Personal Secretary/Bodyguard) working to keep us ***focused*** on whatever action steps we need to take to create what **we** want in the world, whilst also keeping our physical body safe and well, without getting distracted and hijacked by fear.

This all sounds pretty straightforward, right? Like having your own little team inside your head all ready and eager to work for you. So what about the many of us who have tried this 'manifesting thing' before, and wound up finding ourselves frustrated, annoyed and doubting. I know. I've been there! Doing really great for a while...and then *something* goes wrong and you feel like you've slipped right back to the beginning, wondering what happened. Don't worry; there is a reason for this, and a solution to it!

It all comes down to the limiting beliefs I mentioned earlier. Whilst your Genie was waiting patiently for you to discover the fact that you have the power to manifest the life you want, he had to busy himself with *something*, so he's been taking instruction from whomever and whatever you've been listening to. Your parents, teachers, peers, etc... he will have been taking *some* instruction from you too. However, as you weren't aware of how to use your Genie, you will most likely have been giving him inaccurate messages based on your experiences, like for example, 'It's my fault my parents got divorced'... and other negative false beliefs along those lines. Remember, your Genie is impartial and just believes what you tell him.

If your Genie is not fully aligned with your desires, your mind will be in conflict, with part of you (your Divine Creator mind) wanting to go ahead and create the life you want, and another part of you (your misinformed Genie) weighed down with nonsense limiting beliefs about how you're not good enough, or don't deserve it...and other such rubbish. You see how this conflict results in the feeling that *something* is getting in your way? That '*something*' is the faulty programming (beliefs) your Genie received before you realised that **you are able to program him** yourself to get to work at creating the life you want.

So, to be able to make full use of your mind you need to clear out any limiting beliefs that were programmed in during childhood by other people, or that you created yourself before you knew any better, and replace them with positive, empowering beliefs.

The following chapters will show you how to do that. But before we get into that, I'd like to formally introduce you to the team inside your head and describe how you can connect with them consciously.

Your Consciousness

Hey there,

I am your consciousness, or awareness, the part of your mind that you identify with as being 'You', so I go wherever you go.

I'm usually quiet, but can get a little intense at times depending on how and where you direct me. When you're feeling relaxed and grounded you will be more aware of me. In those times, I sit behind your eyes in the centre of your head. So the times you may be most aware of me are during and after a meditation, walking in nature, or just spending quiet time with yourself. Other times you may notice me are when you're really focused in on something. I go wherever you direct me. You can focus me inside, during something like meditation, or outside like when you appreciate nature, or talk to a friend. I'm pretty flexible and can expand or contract. When you feel joy and connection I'm in an expanded state, and when you feel fear and anxiety I'm in a contracted state.

Of course I'm well acquainted with the other three members of the team and visit them often. I'm present when you are communing with your divine mind and receiving messages, ideas and inspiration. I'm also present when you're in your thinking mind, planning things or doing tasks, though you may be less aware of me during those times. I'm also there when you venture into the cave of your subconscious and chat with your Genie.

My time to shine comes when you do the techniques in Part 2 of the book. You can move me to any area of your body. During the techniques you focus me inside to whichever area of the body you're feeling some trapped energy or emotion, and I help you to release it. This is really fun for me because I love to feel you level up in your energy, and this happens every time you release an energy block.

It is very helpful if you try to keep me (and the rest of the team of course) focused on what you're trying to create in your life. Whether that be health, wealth, love, or just anything that makes your soul sing.

Your Divine Creator Mind

Greetings, I am your Divine Creator Mind

The best way to connect with me and to stay connected is through a daily gratitude practice. Taking the time to appreciate the little things in life as well as the big things helps to develop your connection with me, which, in turn offers you access to a creative flow state, allowing your best ideas to come forward. Being connected to me also facilitates the experience of joy in your life. A good way to bring this habit into your life is through using a gratitude journal which over time **trains** your mind to focus on the good things in life. This creates a **habit** of positive focus which is a huge part of the process of manifesting a life you love because **whatever we focus on, we create more of**.

Another way to connect with me is through heart centred meditation. To do this you simply find a quiet place where you won't be disturbed and either sit in a comfortable position or lie down. Then take a few relaxing deep breaths in through your nose and slowly out through your mouth. Do this for a few minutes as you allow yourself to relax. When you're feeling relaxed, move the focus of your attention down out of your head and into your heart centre. If you struggle to do this, you could try placing your hand over your heart to show your awareness where to go. Now begin to imagine that you are breathing in and out of your heart centre. Visualise the breath gently moving in and out of your heart as if your heart is breathing, and then begin to notice any images or thoughts that arise. If your Personal Secretary/Bodyguard is firing out negative or fearful images, don't resist them and don't attach to them just allow them to pass through, paying little attention to them as you focus on allowing the space to open into your divine mind and commune with it. If you receive inspiring images or messages from me, you might like to write them down to act on them later. You can tell where the images and messages come from based on how they make you feel. Messages from me make you feel excited, expansive, inspired, free and often joyful. You may like to share them to encourage and inspire others on their journey. Spending time connecting with me will inspire, refresh, sustain and encourage you. Put connecting with me at the very top of your list of priorities and it will change your life in miraculous ways.

Your Genie

Good day, Master or Mistress,

I am your Genie and I live in a cave inside your head. There's a door between where I live and where Your Divine mind and Personal Secretary/Bodyguard live. There's a window in the door and I can also hear through it, so I'm always listening to what you say and watching what you're doing. I am here to make your beliefs and wishes a reality. I take everything you say literally. I'm a serious guy, and I don't have a sense of humour, so don't tell me self-depreciating jokes! because I'll take them seriously and set to work at making them a reality. Before you knew about me and how powerful I am, I was taking instructions about what you wanted from the programming you received as a child, but **don't worry**. There are ways to open the door and communicate with me and to reprogram me with the right beliefs and instructions needed to create what you want to experience in your life and the world. When you really relax your body and then focus in a relaxed way, you are able to slip open the door in your mind and speak with me.

The techniques in this book show you how to do this. You might need to practice to get really good at it, so be patient with yourself, and know that anyone can do this. Meditation is the perfect practice tool for learning how to open the door and speak to me. You might be surprised to discover the limiting beliefs I've been holding about you, your life and the world, but don't worry; **you can change all of them**. I'm YOUR Genie, here to create the life you want and I can't wait to get started!

As well as opening the door to speak to me via meditation and the techniques in this book, I like you to both tell and show me what you want to create in your life. You need to convince me that you **already have** whatever it is you want to manifest and I'll get to work on bringing it in. This is because we attract people, things and events to us that we're *already* a vibrational match to. The best way to do this is to use your imagination to visualise what you want. Enter into your visualisation using all of your senses. See what you would see, hear what you would hear, smell what you would smell and feel what you would feel. Make the experience as visceral as possible as if you are in the experience. Feel that **you already have** what you want to create, and then hold on to that feeling as you go about your daily life. Think and speak about your desired life as if you're already living it and do all you can do on a practical level to prepare for its arrival. Not in a hurried or stressed way, but in an excited and joyful way, full of anticipation!

Also, really feel into the gratitude you will feel when your dream life materialises. Doing this visualisation gives me very clear instructions about what you want, and I love clarity! Please don't confuse me by using words like 'if' when you think about or talk about your vision. I'm a simple guy, so please keep your message clear. If your Personal Secretary/Bodyguard decides to butt in with doubts or fearful ideas about your vision, just let him know that you don't need his help right now, so he can just go and take a break for a while until you need him for something.

When you take action towards making your vision a reality, I really sit up and take notice. Your action shows me that you're serious. You will notice me working through synchronicities, opportunities and pleasant surprises. I am a Genie after all, so I do enjoy my magic 😜

I'm excited to begin creating with you!

Your Personal Secretary/Bodyguard

Hi, how's it going?

I think you know me quite well, I'm your Personal Secretary/Bodyguard. I'm a bit embarrassed to have been placed in the position of running the show up until now. The 'Boss' position doesn't belong to me, it's not what I was made for, so I'm sorry if I screwed things up for you for a while by getting hyperactive as your bodyguard and scaring the crap out of you every now and then, and overzealous as your Personal Secretary thinking that was my job to 'fix' everything. I was just taking on too much responsibility. I'm much happier working as part of a team with your Divine Mind and your Genie. Just like your Genie, my job is to make your dreams become a reality, and I do a great job of this when I'm working for YOU rather than being hijacked by other people. I get scared and distracted very easily, so what I need from you is to keep me focused on what you want to create and away from what you don't. Basically, I need direction from you. Show me what you want and I'll come up with solutions to make it happen. I don't like to brag, but I'm a really good problem solver! The Bodyguard side of me is great when he's just taking care of your body through exercise, good food, and watching out when you cross the road etc but if you keep placing your attention on things that scare you, the Bodyguard part of me becomes hyperactive and assumes the Boss position in your mind when he doesn't need to. So make sure that doesn't happen by only using him when you need him, and at other times keeping your attention away from what scares you and on what you want to create.

I am a very active member of the team and need to be told to take a break. If you could be kind enough to take up a regular meditation practice, this will give me lots of time to chill out and relax. Over time this will also calm my hyperactivity to the point that I'll be much better able to take my rightful place in the team and much less likely to get distracted and hijacked by fear. I love to work and would much prefer to work at creating what you want to see in the world rather than working for anyone else.

Okay, so with the introductions over, let's explore for a minute how our belief system is created.

Mirroring is the name of a process that occurs during childhood where our parents, teachers, friends, and other people we come into contact with mirror back to us their perceptions of us and our behaviour. Through this process, we develop deep-seated beliefs about ourselves which then go on to form part of our identity, our belief system about who we are and how we fit into the world.

So, we each travel through life carrying a set of beliefs about ourselves and the world we live in. Some of these beliefs reflect the reality of who we are and they serve us; others are negative and unrealistic and keep us stuck in destructive patterns that stand in the way of us becoming all that we could be.

Intuitive, Highly Sensitive people and Empaths often find themselves especially misunderstood as children, which can result in them being left with the belief that there is something inherently wrong with them, simply because they experience and process the world differently to the majority.

It is my intention that by working through this book, not only will you be able to identify and change any negative beliefs that you're carrying about yourself, but that you will also come to know and love your special gifts of intuition and empathy and see how powerfully beneficial they can be in your life and to the world.

So Belief Alchemist was written to help you to:

1. Identify the conscious and unconscious limiting beliefs that are keeping you stuck.
2. Change any limiting beliefs you carry into positive, realistic beliefs that will allow you to move through life with much more ease and confidence.
3. Fully understand your powerfully creative mind and take control of it, so that you can manifest a beautiful life that perfectly expresses all that you are.

A quick note about the Belief Alchemist exercises and techniques

The Belief Alchemist exercises and techniques are found in Part 2 of the book.

It is very important that you take a relaxed, non-judgmental approach to all of the Belief Alchemist techniques and exercises. When using them **do not** look to judge yourself, your beliefs, or your feelings, but rather develop a relaxed approach to yourself that is both focused and curious. The techniques are designed to help you to get to know yourself without judgement and to help you to release emotional energetic blocks. Explore your mind, belief systems and emotions gently, carrying with you a curiosity about what you might find. Please allow yourself enough time and quiet space to carry out the techniques... never rush them... and for safety reasons, never listen to the audio version of the book or techniques whilst driving or operating machinery.

Be sure to read the Belief Alchemist Guidelines before using the techniques and **especially the part on fear**. Almost everybody experiences some degree of fear when confronting parts of themselves they've been trying to avoid, so read the guidelines and take courage. **The fear soon passes** and is replaced by an increased sense of confidence, freedom and joy, so it's well worth the effort!

The more you use the techniques in this book, the deeper your understanding will become of how your mind develops beliefs, and the ways in which your super conscious, subconscious, and thinking mind are serving you. You will also become more acquainted with and accepting of your feelings and how they inform you as messengers of your deepest needs and desires, as well as of what is going on deep within your psyche. This will enable you to get the best from yourself and to make clearer and more confident decisions. So please use the techniques often and be sure to do the quick grounding and awareness exercises before doing each technique!

Inspired Intention is powerful.

At the beginning of each chapter I have written an intention. Creating clear intentions for our lives is not only powerful, but also essential to us remaining on our path and achieving the results we want. Before moving on to each new chapter, read the intention and say it out loud to yourself a few times. Also write it down and visualise yourself having already achieved it. How would you look, feel and carry yourself? Create within yourself an excited expectation of success, as you approach each chapter, but do not rush or pressure yourself. This is a process with its own natural timeline. Trust it and allow it.

Lastly, over the past few years there has been an 'anti-negativity' movement that encourages people to deny, repress, or even shame themselves for carrying negative beliefs or for experiencing negative thoughts or emotions. This is counter-productive to finding self-love and self-acceptance, and is not what this book is about. I believe that we are all expressions of the divine mind, perfectly imperfect, and that we're here on earth to experience, learn and grow. **All emotions are valid and welcome messengers**, not just the positive ones! We experience a spectrum of emotions for a reason, so please do not give yourself a hard time for experiencing the full spectrum of thoughts, feelings and emotions that go with being a fully connected human being.

We're not supposed to be perfect. So, although we are going to focus on clearing out our old mistaken beliefs of unworthiness, the main purpose of becoming your own Belief Alchemist is that you learn to love yourself unconditionally and in spite of your natural human flaws.With all of that said, lets dive in!

Insight - Your Innate Self

Intention: I now shift my focus from looking outwards to the world for approval, to turning inwards to reconnect with myself.

We are all a product of nature (our innate self), of the nurturing (or mirroring) we have received, and of our life experiences. Some of the beliefs we carry about ourselves reflect the truth of who we really are at core and others do not. For the purpose of gaining clarity regarding which of our beliefs are in line with reality, it's important that we reconnect with our innate self. In this busy world where we are constantly being distracted, it's easy to lose connection to who we are at our core. This loss of connection can leave us feeling anxious and confused, as we are no longer able to hear our inner voice and to benefit from its guidance. Reconnecting with who we are is the first step towards changing any limiting beliefs we hold.

To begin this reconnection process, I strongly advise that you begin to journal.

You could either buy yourself a notepad or journal, or create a locked file on your PC, and just begin to record your thoughts, insights, and feelings. This will really help you to connect with yourself on a deeper level and will also help to reflect your progress back to you as you move through this book. There is no need to be regimented about it, it doesn't need to be done every day and should not become a chore. Do it when you feel like it. Take some quiet time to write down any key events or insights that arise in your life. You could also use the written word to explore your emotions around anything in your life that you feel confused about or unclear on.

Writing can be a very helpful way to reconnect and gain clarity. You will be amazed at how cathartic and revealing journaling can be.

Another way to reconnect with your innate self is through psychometric testing. This can help to reacquaint you with your own special talents, skill sets, and way of perceiving the world. There are many psychometric tests available that offer insights into your unique gifts and perspective. Personally, I have found these tests very enlightening and informative and have used them often in my therapy practice.

If you wish to explore your own or other personality type more deeply, you may like to have an official psychometric assessment done. If you're not able to have an official assessment done, you can find many free tests online which, whilst not as accurate as an official assessment, can still offer valuable insights into your personality type. Once you discover your personality type code you can type it into a search engine and find lots of free information on your type, and also online groups where you can meet others who identify as the same type as you do and you can share your experiences with them.

Understanding how your personality type fits in with the rest of society can be an extremely enlightening and validating experience, especially if you are one of the rarer personality types and have not yet discovered a positive frame of reference for how your skills fit into the world. We all have our super powers, and psychometric tests can help you to discover yours.

How Your Beliefs Were Created

Intention: I explore my belief system with curiosity and kindness.

Your current belief system is the sum of...

Your innate self + experiences within your family (your nurturing/mirroring) + your experiences of the world.

Let's now take a closer look at how your belief system was created...

When we are young, we are very open and receptive to learning as we have a great deal of information to process and store. However, young children do not possess the well-developed critical thinking skills that adults do, and are therefore unable to decide (based on evidence) whether what their mother, father, teacher, etc tells them about themselves and the world is true or not, so they simply accept what they are told as being the truth, and store these 'truths' inside their minds forming what will later become their belief system. The underdeveloped critical thinking skills in children also results in them jumping to some wrong conclusions about themselves and the world, based on their own experiences. A classic example being when a child believes that they are responsible for their parents' divorce.

Because parents, teachers, etc. are not infallible they often pass on faulty information to children. Add to that the mistaken beliefs children sometimes develop themselves around experiences, and we are left with a huge amount of grown adults walking around this planet carrying limiting beliefs about themselves that were wired in during childhood and are simply **not true**. Some of these beliefs will be **conscious** and some of them ***unconscious***. In either case, they will be limiting the person carrying them in many ways.

Most of the time during our busy lives we don't stop to question the validity of our beliefs, we just accept them and get on with things. Our unconscious beliefs also go unquestioned because they are hidden away, out of our conscious awareness. It is only when things are not going as we would like that we may begin to question ourselves and start to realise what an incredibly powerful force our beliefs have been in influencing the direction of our lives.

Let's begin by exploring your conscious beliefs, starting with those you developed as a child from being around your family...

Your family is your first experience of being a member of a group. Groups have a collective identity and the people within them have (or are given) individual identities, or roles to play within the group. More positive examples of the kinds of roles that might be assigned to individuals within a family are: The Joker, The Organiser, The Intelligent One.

In families where children are not mirrored in positive, healthy ways, there is always at least one scapegoat. Scapegoats are given a negative identity within the family group and develop negative beliefs about themselves that go along with that identity. Some of the common titles given to scapegoats are: 'awkward', 'difficult', 'too sensitive', 'attention seeking', 'weird' (my personal favourite), or 'rebellious'.

The unspoken (and often unconscious) 'role' of the scapegoat is to allow the other family members to feel better about themselves by comparison.

Scapegoats are chosen for all kinds of reasons. Very often it is just because they are **different** from the other family members, so they stand out in some way, or because they won't buy into and play along with dysfunctional family beliefs and behavioural patterns. However, one thing is certain, Scapegoats are not born, they are made. The role is assigned to them by their family, and the family ensures that they fulfil it.

If you are the scapegoat or black sheep of your family, you may have been convinced that you deserve that role or title, especially when your family selectively cites incidents which in *their* minds justify it. You may have accepted your family's view of yourself as being the truth of who you are. However, **it rarely ever is**, especially in cases of scapegoated children. Remember, you were not born to be a black sheep, or a scapegoat. You were assigned the role and coerced into playing it.

Alternatively, you may have come from a loving family where you weren't scapegoated, but you were quite different from the other family members and felt misunderstood purely due to that. This can also result in the development of mistaken limiting beliefs about yourself.

Whatever your personal story is, exploring and re-evaluating your role in your family, and noticing how it has impacted your beliefs about yourself and the world can be an extremely useful and enlightening experience.

Take some time to consider the beliefs you currently hold about yourself and the world around you, and compare them to your family's view of you. Then enter them on the worksheet entitled Exercise 1: How your beliefs were created (page 116). (Worksheets are found in Part 2 of the book.)

Do you notice any similarities? Can you see how your view of yourself and the world has been influenced by your family environment?

Now read through the Family of Origin Technique (page 101) several times to familiarise yourself with it before working through it. Be patient with yourself and take your time in working through the technique to challenge and change any beliefs you accepted about yourself that were not true and have not been serving you. The more you use the Belief Alchemist techniques, the easier they will become to use

Now consider what you have learned about yourself through using this technique and re-enter your revised set of beliefs about yourself and the world in Exercise 2: How your beliefs were created (page 117).

A Deeper Dive into Your Beliefs

Intention: I now begin to take back my power by reprogramming my Genie with positive beliefs that align with the truth of who I am.

So, we have looked at some of the beliefs you developed about yourself and the world as a result of being around your family. Now let's take a look at other conscious negative beliefs you may be carrying that have been holding you back or not serving you.

Take a few minutes to read through the list below whilst also paying close attention to your *feelings*. As you do so, notice whether any of the listed beliefs cause feelings to arise within you, or whether there are any that seem to jump out of the page at you as being familiar in relation to the way you see yourself.

Enter any conscious negative beliefs that you discover in the 'Limiting conscious beliefs' column on the worksheet entitled Exercise 3: A deeper look at your beliefs.

List of Negative Beliefs

I'm not good enough.
I cannot love.
I don't deserve success.
I'm stupid.
I'll never win.
I'm worthless.
I can't trust anyone.
I'm a nasty person.
I'm ugly.
I'm not normal.
Other people don't like me.
I'm unlovable.
I must try to please others.
I don't count.
I must make it right for others.
I'm not important.
What others say is more important than what I think.
It's all my fault.
I'm bad (dirty, ruined).
It's dangerous to trust.
My body is bad (ugly, dirty, ruined, contaminated).
I must be in control all the time.
I'm damaged goods (broken, defective).
I must rescue others.
I'm guilty.
I'm not wanted.
I can't trust myself.
I'm pathetic.
People can't be trusted.
I'm immature.
I'm not safe.
I am a failure.
I can't be angry.
I must keep people away.
I can't let pain out.
I mustn't let others know what I'm really like.
People will always hurt me.
I'm a disappointment
Hurt other people first.
I will always be betrayed.
I can't be known.
I will always be let down.
To feel is to be unsafe.
I will always be alone.
I'm trapped with the pain.
I can't cope.
I'm out of control. I'm a liar.
I am shallow. I'm strange. I'm a freak. I'm weird.
I'm useless.
There's no escape. I'm clingy.
I'm scatty.
I'm not worth noticing. Life is pointless.
I can't speak up.
I'm not normal.
I will always be on the outside.
I'm not part of the human race.
I'm mad.
I don't deserve love.

I'm unattractive.
I have a horrible personality.
It's unsafe to be still.
I will never have peace.
I am unlucky.
The world is against me.
I don't like myself.
I can't take care of myself.
I'll never be anything.
I will die if I know I can't tell.
I need to protect others.
I can't succeed at anything.
My thoughts are dangerous.
My thoughts are stupid.
I make things up.
I can't tell what's real.
No one can be trusted.
There's no escape.
I'm bound to fail.
I can't change.
I can't help myself.
No one can help me.
I will never be happy.

When you have finished looking through the list, take a few minutes to consider whether you are carrying any additional negative beliefs that were not included on the list.

You may be surprised to discover just how many negative beliefs you have been carrying around about yourself that you were only semi-conscious of. Often, a closer inspection of these beliefs using your rational mind is all that is needed to challenge and change them.

Before you do that though, consider the effect that carrying each negative belief has been having on your life. In which ways have these beliefs been holding you back?

Enter your beliefs and the effect they have been having on your life on the worksheet entitled Exercise 3: A deeper look at your beliefs (page 118).

Now let's take an **objective look at these beliefs one by one**, using your rational mind...

Take your time to slowly go down your list of beliefs asking for each one:

1. Where did this belief come from?
2. How long have I felt this way?
3. Do I have ***substantial** evidence to support this belief?
4. Is it a balanced belief?

5. Does this belief resonate as being true **deep down at my core**?
6. Is it really true?
7. What is the realistic positive truth?

** Cherry-picking warning!*

Be careful when answering these questions that you don't give 'cherry picked' answers. It is very easy to find 'evidence' for something we ***already*** *believe* ***by only focusing on information that supports it****. Make a concerted effort to be objective and balanced when answering the above questions.*

When you have challenged and changed the *conscious* negative beliefs you have been carrying about yourself, complete Exercise 4: A deeper dive into your beliefs (page 119) entering your old beliefs in the left hand column, followed by your new realistic beliefs in the right hand column under 'revised, realistic conscious beliefs'. Notice how much better you feel when moving closer to the truth of who you are.

If you are still having difficulty letting go of conscious negative beliefs despite realising that they are not true on a rational level, try using the Letting Go of Negative Beliefs Technique (page 105). You may need to use this technique several times over a period of time before you feel that you have fully let go of all of the negative beliefs on your list and replaced them with realistic positive beliefs.

Exposing and Changing Unconscious Beliefs

Intention: I uncover, challenge and change any limiting beliefs my sneaky Genie has been hiding from me!

Changing the conscious or semi-conscious beliefs that have been holding you back is one thing, but how do we become aware of unconscious beliefs to be able to challenge and change them? Very often it is the unconscious beliefs that were wired in during childhood that do the most damage. These beliefs are often simplistic and general. They have an unsophisticated, childlike generalisation to them due to the fact that they were formed during childhood inside a child's mind.

The generalised nature of these beliefs is what makes them especially good at keeping you stuck. An example of this kind of belief would be the belief that 'nothing ever works out for me'. Notice how broad and general this belief is, it refers to ALL areas of your life which is what makes it so potentially damaging. If you think about the way children sometimes respond when things don't go as they had hoped, you will see where this black and white way of thinking and forming beliefs comes from.

Now consider how carrying this kind of generalised negative belief could have been affecting your life.

A person carrying a belief that 'nothing ever works out for me' will be...

Walking around day to day carrying an expectation of failure.

They will be going for job interviews expecting not to get the job or setting up businesses expecting them to fail. They will be entering relationships expecting them to fail. In fact, wherever they place their precious time, attention and energy, they will be expecting to fail.

How will carrying an expectation of failure affect this person's life?

An expectation of failure will deplete their physical energy and creativity. After all, why put in that extra effort when you expect to fail? Why become hopeful and excited when you expect to fail?

Through carrying an expectation of failure, they would also be sending out a **strong message** of this expectation to others **unconsciously** through their speech, energy, body language, etc. This will cause other people to lose confidence in them and also to expect them to fail.

So, you can see that through carrying a belief that 'nothing ever works out for me' a person is effectively **setting themselves up to fail**.

Your internal beliefs really are expressed in your outer reality! You see the kind of havoc carrying generalised negative beliefs can wreak in your life? So, what can we do about these unconscious negative beliefs?

Well firstly, they need to be made conscious as you cannot change something you are unaware of, and whilst it is totally possible to uncover them, it will take a little time and patience on your part.

The great news is that clearing your closet of these insidious, crippling beliefs has the capacity to completely change your life for the better, so it's well worth any time or effort you put into it!

Feelings

The way to make these beliefs conscious is to become **aware of and in touch with your feelings**.

In the Western world, we are not taught about the power and value of our feelings.

Instead of being taught how to understand and *learn* from our feelings, we are taught how to ignore them by pushing them out of our awareness using food, alcohol, exercise, relationships, or by distracting ourselves with work.

Our feelings are **not** an inconvenience like we have been taught; instead they are powerful messengers which help to both inform and create our reality... and to ignore them is to ignore one of our most powerful resources.

Our feelings are also **strong indicators** of our **beliefs**.

Our beliefs generate thoughts, and our body responds to those thoughts with feelings. Our beliefs **do not need to be true** to be able to generate thoughts that produce strong feelings, we only need to believe that they are true...

A good example of this is that of a child who believes there is a monster under his bed. This belief generates all kinds of scary thoughts, which then generate unpleasant feelings. His heart starts racing, his hands become clammy, he becomes very scared and starts to cry.

We have all had this kind of experience in childhood, where we strongly believed something that wasn't actually true and experienced powerful feelings of fear as a result of it.

So, there you see the relationship between beliefs, thoughts, and feelings.

Beneath feelings lie thoughts.

Beneath thoughts lie....

The beliefs that generate the thoughts.

Based on this relationship between feelings, thoughts, and beliefs, we are able to access our deep unconscious negative beliefs through exploring our feelings, and then to challenge and change them to realistic, positive beliefs.

The feelings provide a pathway to the underlying belief that is generating them as in the diagram below:

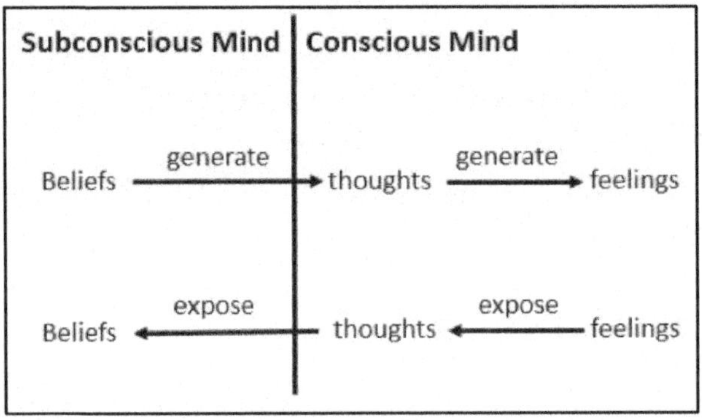

Whenever you find yourself in a situation where your feelings have been *triggered* and you are **overreacting** in some way but are unsure of why, you are likely to be reacting to a limiting belief about yourself that is lurking in your subconscious mind but you are unaware of. Like a sore spot in your psyche that has just been poked.

The uncomfortable feelings you experience offer you the opportunity to explore, challenge and change the limiting belief that caused you to overreact and to change it into a positive, realistic belief that empowers you.

The next time you find yourself in a situation where your emotions have been triggered and are out of proportion to the situation, use the Exploring Your Feelings Technique (page 107) to discover, challenge and change the unconscious negative belief that is generating the feelings.

The more you practice using this technique, the better you will become at being able to access and change any subconscious negative beliefs that have been holding you back. Some beliefs will be harder to shift than others, so

don't be afraid to use the technique as many times as you need to for each belief.

Self-Consciousness

Intention: I hereby kick the butt of self-consciousness and allow my brilliant light to shine for all the world to see.

The way you speak to yourself is of the utmost importance. **Remember your genie, the subconscious mind?** Your genie is ever present, listening to all you say and waiting to fulfill your wishes, so it's very important that you become conscious of the power of your spoken words, so that your genie is focused on creating what you want in your life, instead of what you don't!

Begin to notice your self-talk and the way you speak about yourself to others. Do you validate and encourage yourself? Or do you put yourself down and make disparaging remarks about yourself? Do you judge yourself harshly when you make a mistake? Or do you offer yourself the same kindness and leniency you would a good friend?

Your self-talk has a profound effect on your mind and body! To demonstrate this try the following **exercise**...

Paying close attention to the energy within your body, close your eyes and tell yourself you're no good. Say it several times out loud, bringing in reasons why you believe you're no good. Say it like you really mean it.

Now notice how you feel within your body. Do you feel like your energy has become a bit depleted? Are you feeling a bit heavy or listless?

Now close your eyes and again paying close attention to your energy, tell yourself that you're a great person. Say it out loud several times, like you really mean it, and bring in reasons why you believe you're a great person.

Now notice how you feel within your body. Do you feel slightly energised and lifted?

These **subtle shifts in our energy occur all the time** based on our thoughts and beliefs about ourselves, so it's easy to imagine how exhausting negative self-talk can become over time and how it can lead to depression!

To begin changing your self-talk you first **need to become aware of it**. This requires taking periods of quiet time by yourself without any distractions. Taking walks in nature can be a great way to do this.

As you begin to become more aware of the way you speak to yourself, record the kinds of things you say to yourself on a regular basis on the worksheet entitled Exercise 5: Self-consciousness (page 120). As your awareness of your self-talk grows, you will be amazed to discover how you have been speaking to yourself and the effect it has been having on your energy levels, your self-esteem and your life!

To change your self-talk, instead of putting yourself down, you need to become your own best friend and cheerleader. A powerful way to begin to do this is to think of somebody you respect and admire, and begin speaking to *yourself* the way you would speak to them, offering yourself the same patience, encouragement, forgiveness and kindness.

You will also be affecting your self-talk in a positive way through using the Belief Alchemist techniques that help you to identify and change unconscious negative beliefs.

The habit of negative self-talk can seem difficult to overcome in the beginning, but persistence is the key to success! If you find it difficult to stop listening to your negative self-talk, try the following exercise:

> Imagine that the negative voice in your mind is an actual person who keeps following you around, saying negative things to you and putting you down. Create a funny image of them in your mind and give them a funny name. Now, instead of taking what they say seriously, notice what they say, and then reply 'thanks for your input (funny name) but I don't agree', then use your inner cheerleader to counter what they said with something positive about you and say it out loud. If the negative voice in your head gets nasty or aggressive you can tell it firmly to 'shut up!' Just the same way you would if a literal person kept belittling you and putting you down.

To really re-educate your Genie in the truth of who you are and towards creating the life you want, positive affirmations are extremely powerful and fun to create! The subconscious mind enjoys music, symbols and poetry. So your Genie loves to receive your positive beliefs about yourself in rhyme! Like for example 'Today is a perfect day, abundance flows my way!' You could also add rhythm and music to make the message even more powerful. Creating your own personalised affirmations is powerful because you know best how to communicate with your own Genie. Word your affirmations carefully, as you get what you ask for. You may feel silly to begin with; however, when you realise how powerfully your words affect your life, you will make positive affirmations an important part of your everyday routine.

Recognising and Releasing Victim Mentality

Intention: I release any beliefs around being a victim of life and know that I am the powerful creator of my life.

Living in victim mentality is possibly the most disempowering state to be in. It is a state of ultimate powerlessness. Many people are in this state **unconsciously**; especially those who did not receive healthy mirroring.

If you find yourself procrastinating, feeling stuck and out of alignment with your personal power or you find yourself overreacting to slight criticisms from others, being brought down very easily by the comments or actions of other people...then you are most likely carrying unconscious beliefs about being a victim of life, rather than an empowered creator.

It is impossible to be fully self-confident and in your personal power whilst carrying beliefs about being at the mercy of life and of other people. Whilst it may well be true that in the past you *were* the victim of the thoughtless or even cruel acts of others, it is now up to you as an adult to free yourself from the role of victim by choosing to release the beliefs and feelings that went along with those difficult situations from the past, and to step into your personal power as the master of your own destiny.

Let's consider for a minute how the victimisation cycle works. A person who victimises others has usually been victimised themselves and is attempting to pass on the negative beliefs they developed as a result of being victimised because they don't want to carry the identity they believe goes along with having those beliefs.

So instead of taking responsibility for how they feel and working to challenge and change the negative beliefs they carry, they try to get rid of them by passing them on to someone else.

This may offer them temporary relief, however over time it creates a vicious cycle because every time they victimise another person, they re-confirm to themselves any beliefs they carry about being a 'bad person' which results in an increasingly negative sense of their own identity. Had that person got help, and worked through their painful beliefs, they would have been able to release them and in doing so to preserve a positive sense of who they are, without ever having victimised another person.

Another response to being victimised is to take on the negative beliefs passed on by others and to internalise them. This response is one often taken by empaths who have a natural tendency to soak up the energy of others, and a strong code of ethics on how to treat people. At first glance, this appears to be a painful and self-destructive way of dealing with victimisation; however, it preserves the empaths' sense of decency, and offers them the opportunity of healing when they're ready, without ever having betrayed their code of ethics through trying to pass on their pain to someone else.

We have all suffered victimisation at some point in our lives, and it's never these experiences that define us, but what we do with them. Nobody who is victimised is responsible for the negative energy or beliefs of the perpetrator; however, we are responsible for the way we respond to it. We choose whether to remain in a victim state, carrying that negative energy forward with us throughout our lives, or to release it and let it go in the knowledge that it **never belonged to us** in the first place!

Releasing yourself from the negative energy projected onto you by another person does not in any way absolve the person or people who hurt you, it simply frees you up to be the empowered person you were supposed to be...

So, how do we release ourselves from victim mentality? Well, it starts with becoming aware. We can't change what we can't see.

Begin to notice how you react when things don't go your way. Notice your self-talk, are you making statements like 'this always happens to me' or 'just my luck' etc. Also, notice your reactions when other people do not behave as you would like them to, do your feelings seem proportionate to the situation? Or do you find yourself overreacting a little bit... or a lot?

Take time to explore your feelings and self-talk on these occasions. Are you jumping to conclusions and feeling that nobody understands or likes you due to a slight comment? Are you expecting people to understand you without you having shown them who you are?

To be able to fully release victim mentality, we need to firstly become aware of any beliefs we carry around with us about being a victim of life, rather than a creator. We also need to process and grieve any events from our past where we were victimised, let go of the false beliefs we developed about ourselves at that time, and release the feelings of sadness around those **false** beliefs.

Use the Exploring Your Feelings technique (page 107) to explore any triggers that indicate that you may be carrying beliefs about being a victim. Expose and change any underlying beliefs that you discover.

You may also like to use the Letting Go of Negative Beliefs technique (page 105) to help to release any stuck negative energy around the beliefs you discover.

Shame and Self-Acceptance

Intention: I release shame based beliefs and make self-love my Genie's new religion!

Shame and self-acceptance are *mutually exclusive* which is why it is so important to identify whether you are carrying any shame-based beliefs as part of your identity and if you are, to challenge and replace them with empowering beliefs around your self-worth.

Shame-based beliefs are developed as the result of repeated messaging that simply being yourself is somehow *wrong*.

This false messaging is communicated to us in many ways. In a society that constantly holds up images of the way we are all supposed to look, think, speak, feel, and perceive the world we are all going to have experienced having been shamed in some way, and the simple reason for this is that we are all beautifully and uniquely **different**. This is the way we were supposed to be, and what makes this world so rich and interesting! As much as I love bluebells, I'm very happy that there are so many other varieties of flowers in this world! And it's the same with people.

So many of us have been shamed every time we showed our authentic self just because we didn't fit with someone else's set of preferences, or because it made them feel ashamed for not feeling courageous enough to stand up and be authentic themselves.

I'm here to tell you that you have nothing to be ashamed of and everything to celebrate just for being your incredible authentic self! Always remember, there will only ever be one of you and no one can ever take your place.

The more you begin to release your shame based beliefs, the more you will grow in the strength of your authenticity and self-confidence.

Carrying deep-seated shame-based beliefs causes people to put on a false front to deal with the world. If you are suffering from shaming beliefs, not only will you be carrying the original wound of shame that was created when you were younger, you will also be carrying a sense of shame (perhaps less consciously) due to the fact that deep down you are aware that you are now **betraying your true self** by putting on a false front. So in a sense, you may be operating under a double layer of shame.

As with other limiting beliefs, shame drains our energy on a daily basis and keeps us from our potential. Also, every time we put on a false front and act against our true nature, we are chipping away at our self-confidence. Think about the message you are relaying to yourself through acting against your true nature. You are saying 'I'm not good enough, so I'm putting on a false front which is better or more acceptable than my true self'.

You are reinforcing to yourself the idea that being who you really are is not okay. This is not only painful it is also **untrue** and is keeping you from allowing your unique authentic self to shine! Don't beat yourself up though, this betrayal of self is something we all do to some degree until we feel confident enough to just be ourselves. You will have just been trying to protect yourself and to 'fit in'.

Replacing shame-based beliefs with positive, accurate beliefs about who you are is extremely liberating! Remember your Genie, the subconscious mind? Well your Genie not only responds to the way you talk to and about yourself, he also responds powerfully to the way you **treat** yourself. So as well as working with any shame based beliefs you have been carrying, also begin to take **action steps** towards *expressing* your authentic self, more and more every day. This could be through something as small as just wearing what you like, rather than what's 'in fashion', or speaking your truth to a friend. The more you move in the direction of your authenticity you will find that shame will just melt away, leaving you comfortable and happy to just be yourself.

Use the Shame and Self-Acceptance Technique (page 109) to identify and free yourself from any negative shame-based beliefs that have been holding you back.

Conquering Your Self-Sabotage Mountains

Intention: I gently and truthfully uncover, challenge and change the limiting beliefs I hid from myself under mountains of excuses. 😜

Your self-sabotage mountains are the limiting beliefs that keep you from taking action **and becoming purposeful!**

Carrying negative beliefs about ourselves is painful, so to protect ourselves from experiencing the pain of them, we sometimes cover them over with less painful beliefs or justifications.

Over time, these 'cover stories' we tell ourselves can mount up to the point of completely obscuring the original painful (but false) core belief we were trying to avoid. So although we get to avoid the painful beliefs, the payoff is that over time we find ourselves stuck behind these belief mountains, unable to move past them to achieve our goals, and no longer conscious of what it is that's holding us back because the real reason (the original core belief) is hidden from us at the base of our belief mountain underneath layers of more palatable beliefs and justifications.

Yes! We really do go *that* far to avoid dealing with emotional pain. The Belief Mountain is not a bad strategy to get you through childhood when you're not yet capable of working through difficult emotions, and making sense of them. However, when you're trying to make progress later in life and you keep finding yourself stuck and frustrated, it can become very annoying.

This frustration and annoyance signifies that the time has come to dismantle your mountains and free yourself from the false limiting beliefs that lie beneath them. The great news is that with some focused will power on your part, this is very achievable.

So how do we start to recognise our belief mountains so that we can dismantle them? They are recognizable by the fact that they seem to you like an unsolvable puzzle, something you just can't seem to get over or past and you're not sure why.

Another indicator of a belief mountain is that not only can you yourself not find a solution to the apparent block to your progress, you will also brush aside any solutions suggested to you by other people. In other words, you protect your mountain. Somewhere deep down inside you there is a **resistance** to moving forward because on an **unconscious** level you are afraid to uncover and confront the painful core belief you are hiding from yourself.

Here's an example of a belief mountain **in action...**

'Until I have discovered the purpose of my life, I cannot allow myself to really live fully.'

This is a cover belief. It's what someone may be telling themselves to cover up a deeper, much more painful belief wired in during childhood that, for example...

'I do not deserve a happy life.'

That is a very simple example. Belief Mountains often include several layers of more palatable beliefs and/or justifications overlaying the more painful core belief. But you get the picture.

Another example of a belief mountain might be...

'I'm not going to apply for the job I want because I don't think I'm ready for the responsibility.'

Again, this is the surface belief and of course, it sounds plausible, clear, and logical...but is it really true? Or is it a cover? Something you are telling yourself because in reality, at a deeper level you believe that...

'I'm not good enough to have that job.'

So, you see how this works...

We cover up painful core beliefs with more tolerable beliefs **to avoid dealing with the painful emotions** which accompany painful core beliefs. And whilst **these painful limiting beliefs stay hidden, they keep us stuck in old patterns and sabotaging our lives.**

If you are feeling stuck in your life and you can't understand why it's likely that you will be carrying several disempowering core beliefs about yourself that are hidden from your conscious mind by more palatable cover beliefs.

So how can you change and move past these blocks to your success and freedom?

You can do this by being brave enough to open yourself up to a deeper level of introspection than you've been used to. This will allow you to discover, acknowledge and release even the most painful beliefs you have been carrying, which have been obscuring your view of yourself, and to step into the world freely as the beautiful soul you are.

Try the following exercise:

*As with all of the exercises in this book, set yourself some quiet time where you will not be disturbed, and do not judge yourself for any beliefs or feelings you discover. Remember these beliefs were created when you knew no better.

1. Write a list of areas in your life where you feel **stuck**.
2. Begin to notice and question your thinking patterns around these areas. As mentioned earlier, you can often identify a belief mountain by the fact that you are quite protective of it. If anyone tries to help you to solve it or tries to help you look

at it in a different way, you may find yourself feeling a bit annoyed or defensive. You will have been avoiding directly confronting it, even though you may have been also feeling very frustrated.

3. When you have identified a mountain, relax, close your eyes and gently begin to explore your beliefs and feelings around it by asking yourself questions like:

   'How long have I had this belief?'
   'Where did it come from?'
   'How is it serving me?'
   'How do I feel about it?'
   'Is it comforting in some strange way?'
   'Does it keep me feeling safe?'
   'How realistic is it?'
   'How would I feel if I let it go?'
   'What would I lose if I don't let it go?'
   'What could I achieve by letting it go?'
4. The key to this is honesty. Be sure to be completely honest with yourself when answering these questions.
5. Through gently exploring by asking yourself questions, whilst also paying close attention to your feelings, you should be able to uncover the painful core belief you have been hiding from yourself. You may be surprised to discover how basic, generalized, and wrong this belief is about you. Don't be hard on yourself! We all carry mistaken limiting beliefs from childhood – you're not alone.
6. When you have discovered a belief, challenge and change it by looking at it realistically using your critical thinking skills, and also in light of your life experience, and replace it with what you know to be the truth about you. Do this until any negative feelings around the painful core belief have been replaced by positive feelings generated by the new positive belief. Very often, just the discovery of the painful core belief will be enough to change it.

Self-sabotage as a way of avoiding positive feelings:

As you begin to shed more and more limiting beliefs, you will begin to experience a lighter and more positive state of being. This can be a bit disconcerting to begin with because it feels unfamiliar. It can even feel quite strange and even '*wrong*' to some people, after having been used to carrying a more dense energy. We often associate what is familiar to us as being safe, and change as being a threat.

Due to this feeling of unfamiliarity, some people may try to distract from the new positive feelings, to numb them out, or escape them in much the same way as they might have done previously with negative feelings, using food, alcohol, exercise, or other distractions in an effort to feel safe and in control.

Sensitive intuitive people in particular often experience their feelings very acutely and strongly, and it is understandable that at times they may feel overwhelmed by them, which is why it is very important to allow yourself the time needed to adapt and become accustomed to this lighter, more positive energy.

Another reason that you may try to escape positive feeling states is if you are still carrying *some* negative beliefs. If you feel like *part* of you is resistant to the new positive feeling, check for any remaining negative beliefs around not deserving happiness or joy. If you come across any limiting beliefs, use the Loving Parent part of the Exploring Your Feelings technique (page 107) introduced earlier to correct any of those.

It's important to become comfortable with experiencing positive emotional states without fearing that they won't last. Stay mindful of the fact that feelings carry messages, and this goes for pleasant, positive feelings too. They can signify that you are making the right decisions and that you're on the right path. A good way to become comfortable with positive feeling states is to learn to just sit with the feelings, allowing yourself to notice, but ignore any compulsion to try to distract from them. Breathing can really help with this. Close your eyes and just sit and breathe through the feeling, allowing yourself to fully experience it. When you feel more comfortable, you might like to begin to explore it by asking questions about this positive feeling state, and notice what arises.

Explore any creative thoughts or images that you notice. Our emotions arise with a purpose. They are there to inform and inspire us. Listen carefully to any messages or motivations that the good feelings bring along with them and note them down to act on them later.

Also remember that happiness and joy are great to share, so pass your good feelings forward in any way you can!

It's Great to Be Different!

Intention: I pay attention to and trust the intuitive insights, creative ideas and guidance coming from my Divine Creator mind.

Understanding and Trusting the Intuitive Process

We are all uniquely different from each other. However the current education system does not allow for these differences and puts all children through a uniform rote learning system that suits some, but feels alien to those with a different learning style. Those with a more intuitive learning style, may have found themselves bored or lost at school. If you are one of those people, be in no doubt that you possess a powerful skill set! This may be something you have always suspected, but has been repeatedly invalidated by society as being 'woo woo' and unrealistic. There is so much more to us human beings than the rational thinking mind and this goes for everyone regardless of how intuitively inclined they are. We all possess intuition and we have all been educated out of using it. Learning to take your intuition seriously and to trust it is a very rewarding and self-reinforcing process that will benefit anyone who does it. However, as it goes against everything we were taught at school where linear thinking is king, and everything has to be 'proven' to be accepted as true, it may take time and practice to bring intuition back into our daily lives and use it as it was meant to be used.

Having been talked out of trusting the intuitive part of yourself for as long as you can remember will have had a damaging effect on your self-confidence and ability to make decisions.

Remember that we have three aspects to our mind. The Divine mind, the Subconscious where the Genie lives, and the Thinking mind, our Personal Secretary/Bodyguard. To ignore your Divine mind and Genie in favour of only listening to your Personal Secretary/Bodyguard makes no sense at all.

For you to be able to manifest your dreams, you need to use your whole mind with the Divine mind taking the lead role as the Boss. I heard it said once that prayer is our telephone to the Divine, and intuition is the answer. We ask the Divine for what we want to bring into our lives by speaking it out loud, and then stay alert for the intuitive impulses that come our way and act on them.

Throughout history, there have been many highly successful people who, when asked about their success, attribute it mainly to the fact that they took the time to listen to and **trust** their intuition. Success can show up in many different ways in our lives. However, the overarching truth around success is that it's discovered through honouring our own unique journey with reverence and gratitude, and intuition plays a key role in this process.

Sometimes intuition is experienced as a whisper, a calm, quiet voice in the back of your mind. Other times you may experience it in your body as butterflies in your stomach, your heart leaping or sinking, goosebumps on your skin, suddenly getting the chills, or just an inner sense of knowing... all of these reactions are messages to you from your deepest self to help you to navigate through life.

In the busy times we live in, these intuitive signposts all too often get ignored. People do not stop to notice these messages and warning signs, and even when they do notice them, they often ignore them in favour of the rational thinking they have been trained in.

Those who do stop and take notice of their intuition reap great benefits from listening to it and report that the times when they have ignored their intuitive nudges, things have not gone well for them. Rational thinking *is* an amazing skill; however, if we are to get the best from ourselves, we need to be using **all** of the skills we were born with. Intuition forms a very important part of that skill set and should not go ignored.

To begin to trust in your intuition requires a leap of faith. Below is a list of things you can do to help you to realign with and use your intuition in your daily life.

- Regular meditation.
- Regular journaling.
- Tuning in – closing your eyes and placing your awareness *inside* to access your intuition through asking deliberate questions and exploring goals.
- Trusting your insights. Create an insights and ideas box. Jot down your insights and ideas and put them in a box for future reference.
- Keeping a dream journal. Keep this by your bed to record your dreams upon waking before they fade.
- Tuning in to the energy of a person before meeting them. You can do this by closing your eyes and repeating their name or using a photograph if you have one. This can also to help you to gain a deeper understanding of people you already know.
- Respecting your visions of future possibilities. Take your visions seriously. Create a vision board and begin to work towards fulfilling your dreams.
- Spending time with other intuitive people.
- Spending time in nature.

The Process of Tuning In, or Going Inside

You have been doing this throughout this book when using the techniques. It is simply the process of finding a quiet place, calming your mind and moving your awareness from being stuck up in your head, gently down into your body, so that your awareness fills your entire body from head to feet, and you are able to connect with the deeper parts of yourself.

Meditation can be a great way to train yourself to do this, allowing the breath to act as your guide. I am not going to go into detail on all of the benefits of meditation in this book. However, developing a regular meditation practice is something that I recommend highly and which will help massively when it comes to getting the most from the exercises in this book.

On a side note, if you are suffering from depression and are considering doing some meditation, be sure to discuss this with your doctor.

Intuition in Decision Making

As you gain confidence in using your intuition, a good way to be sure that you are bringing it into balance with your other skill sets is to run any important decisions through the following checklist:

- Intuition - does it intuitively seem/feel right?
- Rational - does it make sense?
- Experience - does it fit with what you know based on your experience?
- Values - does it fit with your values?

You might also like to take a moment to consider your decision making process and the part your intuition has played in it in the past.

Have you been taking your intuition into account when making decisions? Have you been second guessing and dismissing your insights due to not having enough 'proof' of their validity? Have you been allowing yourself to be talked out of listening to your deepest wisdom and instinctive knowing by others who do not value intuition?

Consider and list some of the big decisions you have made over the past few years on the worksheet entitled Exercise 6: It's great to be different (page 121). Consider how you arrived at your decisions, and how they worked out...

Do you see a pattern in how you arrived **at the decisions that worked out well?**

As mentioned earlier, over the last few decades there has been a strong bias in Western culture towards rational thinking and making 'head' decisions, and although things do now seem to be changing so that intuition and emotions are also becoming increasingly more valued in the decision making process, the rational thinking bias still exists. This is not so bad if you are naturally inclined towards making decisions using concrete information predominantly, although you will still be missing key information. But for those for whom rational thinking is not their super power and who naturally lean towards using intuition and heart intelligence as vital components in their decision making process, being forced into using the rational thinking model does not work for them and becomes extremely counterproductive.

Empaths fall into this group and often find themselves in situations where they are being challenged regarding their decision making process so it is very important that they do not allow themselves to be undermined or talked out of their intuitive decisions due to not having enough 'concrete evidence' to support them in the minds of those who do not trust or use their own intuition.

And finally, we all make mistakes! So if a decision does not work out as you had expected it to, don't beat yourself up about it! Consider it as **feedback**, not failure. Nobody's infallible, and making mistakes forms part of our natural growth process, so practice gratitude for the learning you receive from your mistakes and move forward in the confidence that you are making progress.

Consider Your Habits

Intention: It's time to review my habits, and to create new ones that are in alignment with the positive, healthy life I am creating.

There's a very good reason why Steven Covey's book, *The 7 Habits of Highly Successful People*, was so successful, and why Tony Robbins claims to be able to tell a person's habits by taking one look at them. Habits are powerful indicators of our personal belief systems and equally powerful dictators of success.

When a person is carrying negative beliefs about themselves, they are usually also engaging in negative habits. A person's inner emotional and psychological landscape is reflected in the outer landscape of their life.

The reason why negative beliefs result in negative habits is that a person carrying negative beliefs tries to alleviate or numb out the pain of the feelings associated with their negative beliefs by engaging in 'comforting' behaviours or activities. An example of this is comfort eating. The person is not eating due to hunger, but to relieve or distract from uncomfortable feelings.

The problem with this is that while it may make a person feel better temporarily, it does not deal with the *root* cause of the problem (the negative beliefs) and so results in a vicious cycle that offers no lasting relief and often results in the loss of money, health, energy, time, and sometimes, relationships.

Consider your lifestyle and your habits. Are they healthy and productive? Are you engaging in anything which is not serving you like overeating, drinking, overspending, gambling, spending too much time on your phone or on the internet? Anything done to excess is a likely indicator that your inner landscape needs your attention.

The next time you feel the compulsion to do something you know is not good for you, try the following exercise:

Find a comfortable place where you won't be disturbed. Lie or sit down, close your eyes, and take a few deep, relaxing breaths to centre yourself.

- Allow yourself to fully experience and connect with the emotional *energy* driving you to engage in the bad habit and locate the position of that energy inside your body. Do you feel it in your stomach, your head, or your heart? Now take some time to explore and identify the emotion of the energy. It may be fear, anxiety, loneliness, or a feeling of not being good enough. Whatever it is, don't judge it or yourself for feeling it, just sit with it and begin to explore by asking questions about it like:

  'Is this feeling familiar?'
  'Is it a bundle of many feelings, or just one feeling?'
  'When was the first time I felt this?'
  'Where did it come from?'
  'Is there anything underneath this feeling?'

- Sometimes it helps to imagine that the part of you that wants to engage in the bad habit is a separate part of yourself with its own identity, like a separate person. This can help you to fully engage with that particular aspect of yourself and ask it questions like a detective to figure out what specific feelings you are trying to avoid by engaging in the bad habit.

- Try to imagine what this part of you looks like. How does he/she stand? What does their voice sound like? Do they seem young, old, or the same age as you are now? How are they feeling? What do they need?

  When you have identified the emotional drivers that underlie the desire to engage in the destructive habit, begin to identify whether there are any negative beliefs driving those emotions. You can use the Exploring Your Feelings technique (page 107) to do this.
- If you discover any negative beliefs, you can challenge and change them using your rational mind.
- After challenging and changing any negative beliefs you discover, imagine in your mind's eye a scene where the rational part of yourself and the part of you which was driving the destructive habit meet up in a beautiful setting, like in a park, or on a beach somewhere. Then have these two parts of yourself discuss and agree on a healthy alternative to the destructive habit you were engaging in.
- Do this exercise as many times as you need to, to break destructive habits.

Self-Care

Intention: Taking good care of myself has become my number one priority.

Good self-care is essential to happiness and success. If you are not healthy and well, all areas of your life suffer. So make **yourself** your number one priority, and take care of yourself very well. This isn't selfish, as some of us were led to believe, it's practical and smart. It allows us not only to be our best selves, but also to give to others without burnout or resentment. Take a look at the following areas of self-care and notice whether there are areas where you could improve the way you care for yourself.

Diet

I noticed in my therapy practice over the years that Intuitive, Sensitive people and Empaths have sensitive bodies as well as having sensitive minds. This makes sense, especially when considering the research of Dr. Elaine Aron, who suggests that intuitive, sensitive people have a more sensitive nervous system than the average person.

I certainly noticed that many of my clients often complained about chemical sensitivities to caffeine, alcohol, medicines, food additives, etc. As a sensitive, intuitive person myself, I find that I function well and feel at my best when I eat as naturally as possible. I do this by choosing to eat whole, unprocessed organic foods including lots of fresh fruits and vegetables.

I am not a dietitian; however, I have had my fair share of experience of all sorts of different diets over the years, and one thing I know for sure is that we are all very different, with different physical make ups and ancestries. For this reason, I'm a strong believer in figuring out which foods work best for *you* personally within a balanced spectrum of healthy, whole, organic, unprocessed foods that are free from artificial chemicals. The process of figuring out the ideal diet for yourself can take time and patience, but it's well worth it! Getting to know your body in this way enables you to make best use of your energy throughout the day, and helps you to find and maintain a healthy weight effortlessly. Your body really does tell you what it needs and when, as soon as you replace junk food with healthy whole foods, and take the time to listen. Use your will power (your Personal Secretary) to keep you on track, and you will notice that within a relatively short time any addictions to junk food will fade and you'll begin to desire healthy food instead.

Sleep

We are living in a world of chronic distraction and over stimulation, so restful sleep has become even more important than ever to allow our minds enough quiet time to process the huge amounts of input experienced by most people on a daily basis.

If you struggle to fall asleep at night, or are struggling with overwhelm or anxiety due to over stimulation, a good way to begin to calm your mind down is to turn off your phone and computer at least an hour before you go to bed and to dim the lights in the room you are in. In place of these devices, you could read a book or listen to some relaxing music, or you could write in your journal, or just lie quietly, allowing your mind to wander.

Creating a night time ritual is a powerful way of informing your mind and body that it's time to calm down and prepare for sleep.

Try to get at least 7-8 hours of sleep every night and make this a priority. In as much as possible, try to get your sleep during the hours of darkness to maximise your exposure to daylight, as this is also a health-giving practice that helps to balance out the natural circadian rhythms of the body.

Time out

Just as important as sleep, is taking time out during the day to process your thoughts and feelings. Our minds are like in-trays that can easily become overloaded if we don't do this regularly. You know your mind is over loaded when you lose clarity, struggle to concentrate and make decisions, or start to procrastinate and become less productive. You may also find yourself becoming more anxious about life in general and short tempered with others. Any of these things signal that you would benefit from taking some quiet time to yourself.

Taking time out to introspect and to become mindfully aware of your thoughts, feelings, and creative ideas, is so important to allow you to hear the messages coming to you from your Higher Self, or Divine mind, and to act on those impulses to make the most of yourself and your life.

There are various ways you can do this. Some people find that time out in nature really assists this process. Taking regular walks or booking a weekend away in a beautiful, solitary, natural environment can really help a person to get in touch with themselves.

Another method that has been used for centuries by people all over the world is meditation. I cannot stress enough the benefits and usefulness of a daily meditation practice. As well as offering many health benefits (including stress reduction), meditation also helps you to get the best from your mind in terms of clarity. It helps you to be able to see yourself and your purpose much more clearly.

Ethics

Something else I have noticed from working with people over the years is just how important adhering to their core values is to their sense of wellness and self-esteem. It is very important to be fully aware of your core values, your sense of right and wrong, and of what really matters to you. Take some time for a moment to tune into, and write a list of your core values, and to consider how you feel when either you, or someone else in your life does not act in alignment with them.

Acting out of alignment with your own core values not only results in a feeling of discomfort, it also affects your self-confidence. Every time you do or say something that goes against your deeply held values, you are in effect disrespecting yourself by not taking yourself seriously.

So having a conscious awareness of your core values helps to shine a light on what you are doing to your self-confidence if you act out of alignment with them.

Awareness of our values also offers us the opportunity to reassess and change them if necessary. Some people set the bar so high for themselves that their high expectations become a stick that they beat themselves with, rather than being a positive set of guidelines for living life. Being realistic and kind around our expectations of ourselves is essential to our self-care and wellbeing.

Boundaries

I lived a large part of my life feeling like a lighthouse in a storm for people with problems. I drew people to myself unwittingly and unknowingly through the vibration of non-judgmental acceptance I gave off.

Whilst this non-judgmental quality is something I like about myself, it also proved to be problematic to my wellbeing as I found myself constantly drained through listening to other people's problems or being asked for advice, *until* I learned how to set healthy boundaries. Without healthy boundaries, we can find ourselves in situations which drain us to the point that we are useless to ourselves and to others. So being able to assert and maintain healthy boundaries is essential to not only living a happy and healthy life, but also to enjoying happy and healthy relationships.

It's a fact of life that some people have way more empathy than others. Being able to put yourself in another person's shoes is an amazing ability, but it can backfire horribly when it becomes a one-way street.

Some great ways I learned over the years to guard against finding yourself being drained in 'one-way street' relationships are...

Judge a person based on their *actions*. As lovely as words can be, they are only words unless actions follow. Relationships are supposed to be reciprocal.

Give and take. Not I give, and you take. Stay aware of the actions of others and be prepared to withdraw from one-way street relationships.

Learn to say no and mean it. Your ability to empathise could have you jumping through hoops all day long for the sake of making other people happy, and leaving you feeling exhausted and resentful. There is no crime in saying no. We all have our needs, and we all have our limits. If you do not value and take care of yourself, you can't expect anybody else to. When you say no, do it gently but firmly. Do not make excuses for yourself (or other people) and don't get drawn into a dialogue. Just say no and mean it.

Fun!

Make sure you carve out time for yourself to have fun in your life!

Don't buy into the myth that you don't have time, or that it's a waste of time, or that you're 'too old' or any of that nonsense. If you love to sing, do it! Or to paint, or dress up, or dance. Whatever it is that raises your vibration, make time for it. We're here to enjoy life in all its luminous beauty! Now that you have become your own Belief Alchemist, able to clear out the false limiting beliefs you've been carrying, you also get to be your own Life Alchemist and to create a life that resonates with the beauty and truth of who you really are.

Forgiveness and Releasing Judgement

Intention: I set myself free through forgiveness and releasing judgement.

Forgiveness

I couldn't write a book about becoming free and empowered without mentioning forgiveness because it's impossible to become *fully* free and authentic whilst still being tethered down by the energy of anger, hate, rage and resentment that gets passed down from one generation to the next.

As a society we've been taught to hide, deny, repress and push down our emotions. We've been led to believe that displaying emotions is a sign of weakness, and that emotions like rage and anger are unattractive at best, and dangerous at worst. Rather than learning how to process these emotions in safe and healthy ways that allow us to learn from them and move on, we've been shamed for even experiencing them. Experiencing emotions is **not** a sign of weakness; it's an expression of healthy humanity! And the willingness to feel, and learn from our emotions is the hallmark of a courageous, wise and strong human being.

I'm not suggesting that forgiveness is easy. Going through the process of forgiveness can be challenging. It requires us to feel and process painful emotions. It also requires a gentle, but brutal honesty as we meet our own shadow through the process and learn to forgive ourselves for our own mistakes, weaknesses, and potential to do harm.

There's a certain smugness and a false sense of security that goes along with always looking at the person who succumbed to their darker impulses so that we can feel better about ourselves by comparison. It makes us feel good to know that we resisted those impulses, or were never plagued by *that* particular one. However, this sense of superiority and security can only be transient if we truly desire the authentic liberation that is possible for us. Because without searching with courage the darker recesses of our soul, we can never hope to transmute and release the darker aspects of our own nature and to really set ourselves free.

If we don't take this journey of self-discovery, we will remain stuck in the old story that has played out on this planet for centuries. One of victim and victor, where neither stands upright in their authentic power. One where fear is lord and master of all, and love is considered weakness. The ridiculousness of this perspective on life laughs back at us over time, as we move increasingly into the greater understanding that love itself is the force that both created and sustains us. If we are to move into a new way of being in the world we need to be courageous enough to forgive and release the old ways of being.

Let's explore for a moment the alchemy of forgiveness:

We know that fear lies at the root of all offences committed by one person against another. Any attempt to take power over another person is an expression of a feeling powerlessness on the part of the perpetrator on some level.

When we stand in our authentic power, we have no need to try to take power over someone else because we are full of our own power, and as such do not feel threatened by other people.

When we forgive those who have hurt us we demonstrate both to ourselves and them that we are bigger than our experiences. We mirror back to ourselves our strength and resilience.

No one ever does anything without an onlooker. Your Genie is ever with you, ever watching and waiting for you to show him who you are so that he can work towards helping you to fulfil your true identity. Allowing yourself to forgive others sets up a feedback loop within you that allows you to have more kindness and compassion for yourself, and to forgive your own mistakes more easily. This demonstrates to your Genie courage, strength and maturity.

It's the unwillingness to allow ourselves to experience and release painful emotions that keeps the trauma cycle that threatens to destroy our world in motion. So let us pattern interrupt this cycle! Firstly through processing and releasing our own trauma, and then through helping others to do the same.

Unforgiveness only leaves you stuck in victimhood from where it's impossible to really live. When we find ourselves unwilling to forgive another person, we are in effect agreeing to remain in an energetic holding pattern with that person. They have a hold on us. We are allowing them to hold us gridlocked in the energy of victimhood, keeping us from stepping into our full authentic power.

It is forgiveness that allows you to release yourself from the story of your past to create a new life full of amazing possibilities.

Forgiveness is the most powerful act of liberation there is. It's also an act of supreme courage because when you *really* let go of blame for all that's wrong in your life all you're left with is yourself, leaving you suddenly fully responsible for your life. So you are left both liberated and responsible. This is true adulthood and true empowerment.

Forgiveness does not absolve the other person of responsibility for whatever they did. What it does do is to release *you* from living in the energetic state of **victimhood**, this sets you free to fly high.

Genuine forgiveness is not simply a decision; it's a process that *begins* with a decision. It has its own stages and its own timeline, both of which need to be honoured. A person should never be pressured or coerced to forgive; it's a personal decision that needs to be respected. If you decide to take the journey, don't try to rush it. Trust in your Divine mind to guide you through the process. It knows what to do and how to do it.

On a collective level, forgiveness is essential to the continued survival of our species. As we forgive and release the old energies of violence, competition and war – all of which have their roots in fear – we make way for the birth of a new world, one of compassion, creativity and cooperation, all of which have their roots in love and have the capacity to not only save our planet, but also to create heaven on earth.

Whatever happens to us in life, there is always something that can be learned from it. One of the most powerful lessons we can all learn from things that try us is how resilient we are for having got through them. Challenging times reflect our strength back to us like a mirror, often strength we never knew we had.

We are bigger than the experiences that challenge us. So instead of fearing your emotions, allow them to move through you, trusting the alchemical processing of them to mirror back to you anything you need to learn, and most of all what a courageous and beautiful soul you are.

We all intuitively know that it takes strength to forgive and that the larger the offence committed against us the more strength is required to forgive.

So dare to step up and play your part in the very necessary evolutionary shift happening on our planet right now. Have the courage to forgive, setting yourself free to be the huge, beautiful and unique spirit you were born to be, taking full responsibility for the life you've been blessed with and making all you can of it!

It's time for a new story, a new way of being in the world. If we are to create a new story, it needs to be born out of a different energy and belief system than the one that brought us to where we are now, and forgiveness is a very necessary part of this uplevelling.

Rage, Anger and Grief

Processing painful and difficult emotions in healthy and safe ways is essential to the process of forgiveness. Refusing to process painful emotions results in feeling stuck and blocked in life, and can manifest in physical illness. I'm just going to briefly touch on a few ideas on how and where to do this that have worked both for myself and my clients over the years.

There are many cathartic ways to express emotions:

Anger letters where you allow yourself to express your emotion through the written word and then dispose of the letter in whichever way you choose can be a very effective way of allowing anger that has been stuck in your body for years to come up and be released.

Another method is through beating a pillow as hard as you can whilst expressing yourself verbally.

Nature is a very powerful and nurturing space, and private spaces in nature can be great places for you to release anger.

Art is also a very powerful medium for releasing emotions, be it painting, drawing, singing, or writing poetry.

You may want to express yourself verbally within the safe space of a therapy setting, or with a trusted friend or partner.

Whatever ways you choose to express and release painful emotions, make being kind to yourself throughout the process your priority. Don't allow any internalised judgement or shame around expressing 'negative' emotions to get in your way. Kindness and self-acceptance will allow you to move through the process much more smoothly.

Releasing Judgement

My own experience is such that the more I clear out old beliefs about not being good enough, which were based on false negative judgements of myself by myself and others, the more clearly I see myself as I am – acceptable and worthy of love simply because I exist. As a result of seeing this truth I feel stronger, more peaceful, less fearful and much freer. This sense of relief and freedom then extends itself to anyone I meet. I find myself being much more open and accepting, and way less judgemental. This offers me the opportunity of seeing the best in others which massively expands and increases my quality of life.

As you are able to release more and more limiting beliefs and self-love begins to become your natural disposition, you will find that the way you perceive others begins to change also. Self-acceptance and self-love give us the strength to be able to forgive past hurts and also we find ourselves more accepting and less judgemental.

I'm not suggesting that we stop using discernment or boundaries in our interactions, both of which are very important, just that we stop using the judgement of others as a way of either trying to make ourselves feel better by comparison, or to try to make us feel safe. I used to believe that my opinions about other people were keeping me safe. That I needed to be able to 'work people out' to stay safe in the world, but this was not true. This false belief was actually keeping me small and isolated rather than expanded and connected.

Judging others does not keep us safe, it keeps us imprisoned in fear. It's an expression of fear. It stops us from opening up to the possibility of really getting to know someone, and more importantly from really getting to know ourselves as free, empowered beings.

Part of the process of developing healthy self-love is the releasing of self-judgement and the judgement of others. This is an act of strength that is born out of the strength of love. It feels first like a great relief and then like a great joy.

Who would you be if you stopped judging yourself and others and just took people for who they were on a moment to moment basis?

If you really believed that you're good enough and worthy of love just because you exist, what would your life look like? What would your relationships look like?

Aspiring to Be Your Authentic Self

Intention: Loving myself and being true to myself has become my daily habit.

The true authentic you!

This next section deals with gaining more insight into your true nature and potential.

We often get little intuitive flashes of the way we would like to be, or the life we'd like to be living. However, instead of taking these insights *seriously*, we dismiss them as unrealistic or unattainable, or we allow others to talk us out of them. Instead of listening to and taking our deepest desires and inspirations seriously, we look outside at what other people are doing, or at what we believe we are 'supposed' to be doing.

The domino effect of clearing out our negative belief closet is that it clears the lens with which we see ourselves and the world, allowing us to wake up to the fact that the fulfilment of our dreams is not only entirely possible, it's what we're here to do.

We no longer have to dismiss or deny the possibility of the kind of life our soul has been longing for. All we need to do is to place our focus on our dreams in the belief that we can make them happen, and take action towards them a little more each day. All it takes for you to be able to make your dreams come true is desire, focus, action and belief.

At school we were taught to only trust our reasoning mind, and to ignore our intuitive insights unless they could be 'proven'. This is nonsense and leads us down a very narrow and limiting path. All of the greatest scientists, artists and mathematicians in history used their intuition. The rational mind was used as a secondary tool to try to find a way to make use of what they *intuitively felt was true.* Science is still very limited. We still don't even understand how we operate as human beings, so to use science as the only arbiter of the truth to the exclusion of all other resources makes no sense. The intuitive, creative parts of you are the real experts on what is **true for you** as a unique individual, and need to be heard and taken seriously. It's only when you start to take your intuition and inspirations seriously that your true calling and potential will come into focus and your place in the world will become clear to you.

Through consideration of the following questions, and moving forwards in the direction of the answers you receive, you will begin aligning yourself with your natural talents and in doing so, your energy will begin to flow more naturally with a sense of effortlessness.

We all possess skill sets which lend themselves to creativity and innovation in some way or another, and engaging these skills in ways that also align with your values can result in a deep sense of satisfaction and joy that some people describe as being engaged in their calling, and I would call living true to their divine design.

In my therapy practice, I noticed that many people come into their own a bit later on in life. I believe that this is partly due to the 'one size fits all', and 'rational thinking is king' approach of the Western education system, and partly due to the mistaken negative beliefs carried around for many years by most people from childhood. It doesn't matter what age you are, it's never too late to become your authentic self and to become a shining example for others to do the same. Ageism is as ridiculous as believing that science has all of the answers we're looking for, so don't buy into it, and do not let it stand in your way.

Another reason why some people may come into their own later on in life is because it can take a few years to really develop their particular skill sets to the point at which they are fully ready to offer to the world. An example of this would be somebody who's primary skill is in being a great researcher. This person may take several years gathering information before feeling that they're ready to share in a meaningful way like for example, by writing a book.

We are all very capable of learning new things. However, it's important to determine and own *your* particular set of super powers, as opposed to trying to be or do something that doesn't resonate with who you are at your core. Determine your skill set, and then discover creative ways in which you can offer it to the world.

Use the following set of questions to help you to gain more insight into your superpowers...

Consider the following:

When in a positive state of mind, what is the natural focus of your mind?

- Does your mind naturally seek to solve problems?
- Does it like to create fantasies and stories?
- Does it like to explore relationships between people?
- Does it like to generate ideas?
- What does your mind like to do for fun?
- What's its natural direction?
- **What causes your spirit to wake up, sit up and take notice!**

Noticing what energises you helps to discover your natural talents...

When using your talents, you will feel energised and inspired. When forcing yourself against your natural abilities, you will feel resistance and will lose energy and motivation.

To help us to move towards our potential in any area of our life, it is useful to develop some positive habits. A highly effective positive habit is to spend some time each day in envisioning our goals.

Visualisation is a very powerful tool which can help you to both determine your goals and to move towards them. When used regularly and mindfully, the Authentic Empowered Self Technique (page 111) has the potential to change your life! Make visualisation a frequent and fun part of your daily routine. It's a powerful practice to visualise yourself having already achieved a goal as you drift off to sleep at night. This informs your subconscious mind (your Genie) of what to work on as you sleep.

Use the Authentic Empowered Self Technique daily and record any positive changes you begin to notice as you move towards becoming your authentic self!

Planning a Positive Future

Intention: I now use the whole of myself in alignment with divine energy to creative a life I love.

Moving towards your goals becomes **so much easier when you are coming from a place of positive authentic energy and are no longer held back by fears associated with the false limiting beliefs you carried previously. Having your conscious and subconscious mind aligned with your Higher Self (or Divine mind) opens up the path of least resistance for you to move forward because now you are aligned with the truth of who you really are.**

There are many creative ways to encourage and hold this alignment within yourself, below are just a few of them...

- Start each year by writing a list of your goals and aspirations. These could be physical, emotional, intellectual, or spiritual goals.
- Refer to your list often to assess where you are on your journey.

- Create a vision board where you can display pictures and words associated with your goals in a place where you will regularly see it.
- Write down your goals and inspirations on a piece of paper that you carry around in your pocket.
- Give thanks for and visualise yourself having already achieved your goal as you drift off to sleep at night, and when you wake up in the morning.
- Use the Best Authentic Self Technique often! Being sure to **really feel into the emotions** associated with being your best authentic self and achieving your goals.

Don't be afraid to dream big! Bearing in mind the powerful effect positive beliefs can have on your life. However, be gentle with yourself, and move towards your goals at a pace that is healthy for you so that you do not burn out and are able to enjoy each day. Just doing one thing towards your goals each day is progress.

PART 2

Belief Alchemist Technique Guidelines

Fear

Many people experience a fear of exploring and examining their beliefs and feelings, especially unpleasant feelings which they have been doing just about anything to avoid! Remember that your feelings are there to offer information about your internal landscape, and to offer specific information about your beliefs. The negative beliefs we carry from childhood as a result of faulty mirroring are untrue and through exposing and changing those negative beliefs we also rid ourselves of the negative feelings that accompany them. During this process you will need to experience the negative feelings **temporarily** as you explore them to uncover mistaken beliefs. Whilst this is only a temporary thing, it can sometimes be draining so be sure to take it easy on yourself as you go through the process. Take it at your own pace, get plenty of rest and take time out to relax and enjoy yourself in between doing the exercises and techniques in this book. Do not try to 'fix yourself' as soon as possible by rushing through the book or overdoing things, as this **will not work**. Your mind and body need time to assimilate and to integrate changes and new information. Be kind to yourself and take things at a comfortable pace.

Grounding and Awareness

For us to be able to release emotional energy blocks in our body, we first need to be present and focused in our body. We also need to feel grounded. Before using the techniques in this book, I have added a grounding exercise and an exercise to help you to focus your consciousness inside your body. Please be sure to do both of these brief exercises before moving into the techniques as they will greatly improve your experience and results.

Grounding Exercise

Your root chakra is located at the base of your spine. It serves as your connection to the earth (see image above). It roots your physical body to this physical earth. Grounding yourself offers you a sense of security and strength and of being in the here and now.

It's important to ground yourself before moving into any of the Belief Alchemist techniques. Use the following exercise to ground yourself. You can do this either sitting up, or lying down in a quiet place where you won't be disturbed. It may take a few minutes to ground yourself, so take your time and don't rush it.

Take a few relaxing deep breaths, and then move your attention to your root chakra at the base of your spine. Then imagine a thick tree trunk growing from your root chakra deep into the ground with a large root system moving deeply down into the soil. You may notice that your body begins to feel heavier and more solid as you experience the feeling of being connected securely to the earth.

Awareness Exercise

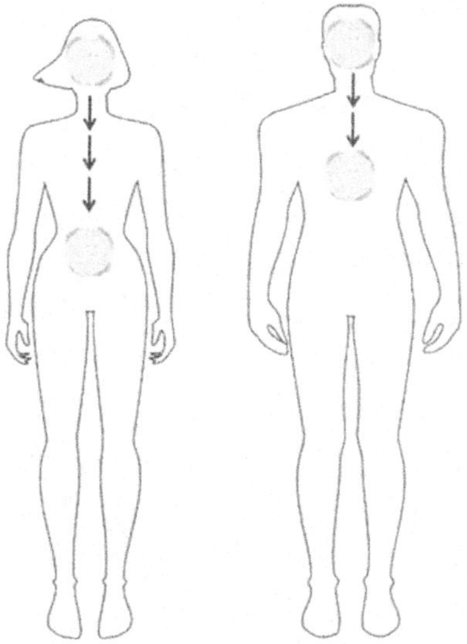

Gentle, but focused awareness is a necessary part of using the Belief Alchemist techniques effectively. With our busy lives, full of distractions, we often find our awareness being pulled all over the place, making concentration challenging. Use the following exercise before moving into the Belief Alchemist techniques, and you will find them much more effective.

Close your eyes and begin taking relaxing deep breaths. As you breathe in, visualise yourself drawing your energy inwards, as if you were gathering any distracted, unfocused energy in from the world and back into your body. Do this for a few moments and then allow your awareness to settle behind your eyes in the centre of your head. From this position you can then practice moving your awareness from the centre of your head down into other areas of your body, like to your stomach area, or to your heart area and notice how that feels.

During the techniques, you will be asked to move your awareness to any areas of the body where you feel trapped emotional energy, to enable you to release it. So practicing moving your awareness to different parts of your body is a helpful exercise to prepare you for the techniques.

Helpful Tips for the Use of Belief Alchemist Techniques

- Always use the Belief Alchemist techniques in a safe environment. Never listen to the audio version of the book whilst driving or operating machinery.
- Read the technique through a few times before using it.
- It can sometimes take a few goes before you feel comfortable using the techniques. Don't be discouraged by that, you are learning new skills and just as with practical skills, psychological skills can also take a bit of practice.
- Be sure to set enough quiet time aside where you will not be disturbed or interrupted. To be most effective, the techniques require relaxed concentration, so always begin with the grounding and awareness exercises.
- Remember to take a curious, non-judgemental approach to yourself as you work through the techniques. Do not judge yourself for any feelings you experience or beliefs you may have been carrying.
- If you find that on some occasions you are unable to 'get into' the technique that day, don't beat yourself up or pressure yourself, just leave it and try again later or on another day.
- Use the techniques as often as you need to. There is no set amount of time by which you should be finished with this book. Everybody has their own pace... respect yours.

Belief Alchemist Techniques

Family of Origin Technique

This technique is not about blame. It's about releasing negative beliefs and energy that don't belong to you, and replacing old beliefs with realistic positive beliefs.

Before using this technique, do the grounding and awareness exercises at the beginning of Part 2 of the book.

- Find a comfortable place to either sit or lie down where you will not be disturbed.
- Close your eyes and begin to take deep relaxing breaths. Do this for a few minutes until you feel your body relax, allowing your mind to become focused.
- Now take some time to consider your role in your family. How does your family see you? What words do you think your family would use to describe you? Imagine a reporter interviewing different family members and imagine what they would say about you if they had to sum you up.
- Whilst doing this exercise, pay *close attention* to your feelings as you visualise your family members expressing their beliefs about you. **Your feelings are strong indicators of any beliefs you may have taken on about yourself.** Also notice any repetition of words or phrases used by your family members. Are they all repeating the same thing about you, as if reading from a pre-prepared script? Just because a group of people may be united in their

opinion of you, this does not make their opinion true. Families often have shared opinions, as this is typical group behaviour. Families who scapegoat hold shared negative opinions and behave like playground bullies in that sense. They share a view, not because it's true, but because it serves them in some way, often allowing them to feel better about themselves by comparison.

- Notice your feelings around your family's view of you. There may be feelings of sadness, frustration, or anger arising within you. Allow any feelings to just be present. Don't judge the feelings, just *allow* them. Notice them and name them. You may feel hurt, misunderstood, angry or sad. Allow these feelings to rise to the surface and release themselves. They may bring some tears along with them. Take your time to allow any emotional release that comes with acknowledging and experiencing the feelings.
- Now consider from your own perspective what your family had to say about you. If the feedback from them was a little negative, consider whether you think it was fair and reasonable, factoring in the way your family have behaved towards you as individuals and also as a group. Bear in mind that nobody can expect sweetness and light from anybody they didn't treat well. Do your family's beliefs about you **ring true** with what you know **deep down** to be true about yourself? Decide for yourself what you believe is really true about you, and what isn't. Unfortunately, there are many people who go through life, never recognising and healing their own inner wounds. Sadly, these people often project the things they don't like about themselves (along with their inner pain) onto other people, including their children. Take some time to consider whether this has been the case for you within your family. Have you been wrongly accused, labelled or blamed for problems that actually belong to other people?
- Take a few more deep breaths and imagine yourself standing in a pleasant outdoor place. You may be in a field or on a beautiful beach somewhere with the sun shining and a gentle

breeze blowing. You are feeling confident, grounded and ready to deal with any negative beliefs you've been carrying from your family. Imagine your family members standing about 30 feet away from you. Call to mind a negative belief your family holds about you that does not ring true to you and become aware of your feelings around this belief in your body. Notice where the emotional energy is situated in your body and move your awareness into this place. Whilst retaining awareness of the emotional energy around this belief, imagine taking the belief and placing it into a large open box. As you do this, allow the emotional energy you have been carrying around this belief to flow out from your body and into the box. At the same time, repeat out loud to yourself, 'This is not my truth. I now release all false negative beliefs and the dense energy that surrounds them.'

- When the emotional energy around this belief has left your body, close the box and visualise yourself giving it back to the family member that belief came from. If you are unsure of exactly where it came from, just lay the box in front of your family. The belief is no longer a part of your identity. * Laying the box in front of your family does not burden them with the belief or the negative emotional energy around the belief. It offers them an invitation to clear this energy within themselves.
- Now that the energy around the negative belief has left your body, consider what the real truth is about you in relation to that belief. Take some time to feel into what is really true about you. What is your new, realistic, positive belief about yourself? Repeat this new belief out loud several times. Notice how it makes you feel and enjoy the new positive feelings in relation to yourself.
- Repeat this process from the beginning for each negative belief in turn. When you have finished, see your family gathering up the boxes and walking away into the distance. Those beliefs are now gone from you and are no longer your responsibility.

- Now bring to mind a person who knows and really values you and imagine that a reporter is interviewing this person and asking them to describe you. Notice the words and phrases this person uses to describe you, the look in their eyes and the tone of voice they use when talking about you. Again, notice any feelings arising within you in relation to this person's positive beliefs about you, and name those feelings. You may feel relieved, happy, appreciated and understood. Notice how relaxing and peaceful it feels having been seen, appreciated and understood for who you really are, and allow this relaxed, peaceful feeling to spread throughout your body, from your head, right down to your toes! It feels great to be seen and understood for the truth of who we really are.
- If you were assigned a negative role within your family, you don't have to accept it. You can begin changing the way your family perceives and treats you by gently setting boundaries around the way you'd like to be treated. There's a lot of wisdom in the saying 'We teach people how to treat us'.
- Visualise yourself setting a boundary with a family member whom you find difficult. See yourself in your mind's eye standing upright and feeling calm and grounded as you gently, but firmly express your wants or needs to this person. When setting boundaries, it's important to keep calm. Do not be drawn into long discussion and do not keep repeating yourself. Say what you have to say calmly and firmly and then leave the situation. *In some cases boundary setting does not work and in those cases having no contact with certain family members may be the healthiest and best option.

Confirm the new positive beliefs about yourself gained from using this technique to yourself often. Say them out loud to yourself and enjoy the positive energy that goes along with having a realistic impression of who you really are!

Letting go of Negative Beliefs Technique

As you work through this technique, **take your time** with each belief. If you feel that you only wish to process one belief each time you use the technique, that's fine. If you have time to work through several beliefs in one session, that's fine too providing you don't rush the process. You may just use the technique once for each belief, or several times over a period of weeks or months. Be led by what works best for you.

- Before using this technique do the grounding and awareness exercises at the beginning of Part 2 of the book.
- Find a comfortable, quiet place where you will not be disturbed and either sit or lie down.
- Close your eyes and take some deep relaxing breaths. Do this for a few minutes until you feel your body relax, allowing your mind to become focused.
- Now imagine yourself sitting or lying in a beautiful, natural setting. It could be by the sea or out in the countryside somewhere. Notice the sights, smells, and sounds all around you. Take a few minutes to just breathe in and enjoy your environment. You are feeling relaxed, calm and open.
- Now imagine a large container beside you on the ground. It could be an old chest, or a clay pot, whatever comes to mind. This container is going to receive the old negative beliefs and emotional energy that you've been carrying.
- Each of the negative beliefs you carry about yourself will have emotional energy attached to it. It may only present as a very subtle feeling, so pay close attention to the sensations inside your body as you work through this technique.
- Slowly work through each negative belief using the following method.
- Think about the belief you're going to work with. Say it out loud a few times and allow yourself to become aware of any negative emotional energy that goes along with it.
- Place your awareness into the area of your body where you feel the negative emotional energy surrounding this belief

and assign a colour to the energy. Don't think about it, use the first colour that comes to mind.

- Now, begin to gather this belief energy within your body to one central point, it could be in your solar plexus area, or in your base chakra, wherever feels right for you. Take your time to allow the coloured energy to gather, and when it feels concentrated in one place, say out loud 'I release the mistaken belief that (fill in the blank) and all of the emotional energy that went along with it. This belief does not belong to me. I release it now.' As you do this, visualise the old belief and all of the negative emotional energy surrounding it flowing out of your body as a coloured mist and down into the container. It may flow out on your breath as you exhale, or it may rise up out of your body and flow out that way, whichever feels right for you. There may be some emotional release in the form of tears or sighing. Take your time with this, until all of the negative emotional energy around the belief has been released and you are feeling peaceful.
- Now consider what you believe is the real truth on the subject of the old belief. What is your new, positive belief about yourself? Say your new belief out loud several times to confirm it, and as you do this, allow yourself to experience the positive energy that goes along with the new belief.
- Allow your mind to assign a colour to this positive energy and visualise this colour filling your body!
- Now imagine that you are closing the container that received your old belief and taking it to a place where you're going to let it go. It could be a cliff top where you're going to drop it over the edge. Or you might want to throw it into the sea, whatever comes to mind. As you release the container full of your old belief, allow yourself to experience the lightness and relief that go along with releasing dense energy.
- Now imagine walking away into the sunshine feeling lighter, brighter, and more positive about your future.

- Keep a list of your new positive beliefs in a place where you will regularly see it. You could write them on your bathroom mirror or on a piece of paper that you carry around with you.
- **Affirm these new beliefs often to yourself by saying them out loud. Remember, your Genie is listening!**

Exploring Your Feelings Technique

This exercise is particularly useful when you feel that someone has pushed one of your buttons and you may be overreacting, as this often indicates a painful limiting belief hiding away in your subconscious.

Before using this technique do the grounding and awareness exercises at the beginning of Part 2 of the book.

- Find a comfortable, private place where you won't be disturbed and either sit or lie down.
- Close your eyes and begin to take deep relaxing breaths. Do this for a few minutes until you feel your body relax, allowing your mind to become focused.
- Access the feeling you would like to explore in your body. If it's not currently present, you can access it through memory. You do this by remembering the last time you felt the feeling. Remember where you were, how you were sitting or standing, who else was there, what you saw, what you heard and how you felt. Recall the event in **as much sensory detail** as possible. Recalling sensory detail helps you to be able to reaccess the feeling.
- When you have accessed the feeling, notice where in your body it is located. Is it in your throat, stomach, chest, or another area? Move your awareness to the part of the body where you feel the feeling. Then, whilst **retaining an awareness of the feeling**, begin to ask questions about it like: 'What is this feeling?' 'Is it familiar?' 'Do I recognise it?' 'Have I felt this feeling before?' 'When did I first feel this feeling?' It is **very important** that you don't judge the

feeling, or yourself for having it. Just allow it to be what it is as you continue to explore it. Think of yourself as a diver with a flashlight strapped to your head and the feeling as the sea. You retain an awareness of the feeling (the sea) whilst using your mind (the flashlight) to explore it.

- Be gentle. Don't push for answers; just allow your mind to offer you what it has. At first you may get superficial information about the feeling, but *keep gently exploring deeper* by asking more probing questions about the answers you receive like, 'And what's beneath that?' For example, if initially the word 'anger' comes into your mind, then ask the question, 'What's beneath the anger?' You may find through exploring more deeply that fear lies beneath the anger, and sadness lies beneath the fear, and so on until you discover a limiting belief. For example, 'I'm not good enough'. You can sometimes discover a limiting belief by asking the question: 'What does this feeling mean about me?'
- Limiting beliefs about yourself that were developed during childhood can be recognised by the fact that they tend to present in the form of blunt, broad, general statements like ' I'm not good enough' which, when questioned using your rational mind, are clearly untrue.
- When you have discovered a limiting belief, you can challenge and change it using what your rational mind knows to be the truth.
- To do this you will need to remain in your relaxed position with your eyes closed whilst still retaining an awareness of the feeling in your body.
- Imagine you're in a pleasant outdoor place like a park, or a beach, or a hilltop. Now place your awareness on the feeling inside your body and imagine that the feeling is the child part of you. The part of you who developed the limiting belief in the first place. Allow yourself to really **connect with this child part of you**. Notice how old they are, what they're wearing, how they're presenting themselves inside your mind's eye. Now you've connected with the child part of

yourself, begin to visualise the adult part of you as being a mature and loving parent, and allow yourself to connect with the strength, stability and kindness of that part of yourself.

- Now in your mind's eye imagine the child part of yourself meeting up with the loving parent part of yourself in the beautiful outdoor place and expressing the limiting belief you have been carrying to the loving parent. Allow the child part of you to fully express how you feel about the belief and the effects of carrying it, whilst the loving parent part of you just listens.
- Then, have the loving parent part of you gently challenge and change the belief that the child part was carrying, explaining why it is not true **and reassuring the child of all their good qualities**. You might also like to comfort and reassure your child part by giving them a hug and telling them that they are loved by you unconditionally.
- When you sense that the child part of you feels relaxed and peaceful, imagine that part of you gently merging together with your adult self.
- Take a few moments to allow yourself to absorb and reflect on the experience of using this technique.

Shame and Self-Acceptance Technique

Before using this technique do the grounding and awareness exercises at the beginning of Part 2 of the book.

- Write a list of all of the things you can think of about yourself that cause a feeling of shame to arise within you.
- Take a look at the list and carefully consider each thing that you feel shameful about, as to whether it *is actually* shameful in and of itself, or whether it simply forms a natural part of your personality that you have been made to feel ashamed of by others, or that you yourself are *judging* as being shameful. Often intuitive, sensitive people have at times been made to feel ashamed of their sensitivity, intuition, or empathy, all of

which are very valuable skills, not something to be ashamed of.

- When you have identified the things on the list that are merely aspects of your character or skill set but that you've been feeling shame around, find a comfortable place where you will not be disturbed and either sit or lie down.
- Close your eyes and take a few deep, relaxing breaths until you feel your body relax and your mind become focused.
- Now bring to mind one of the aspects of yourself that you have been feeling shame around and allow yourself to notice and experience any emotional energy around this aspect of you. Bring your awareness to the place where this energy is situated in your body. As you do this, allow an image of the child part of yourself to begin to emerge from your subconscious mind into your conscious mind. Notice the age of this child part of you, how they are dressed, how they hold themselves and the expression on their face. This is the part of you that has been carrying the feelings of shame.
- Take a moment to experience and acknowledge the feelings arising within you as you focus on this particular aspect of yourself that you've been feeling ashamed of and explore for a moment how feeling shame around this aspect of yourself has been affecting your life.
- Now bring to mind an ideal parental figure. This person loves and accepts you just as you are. They celebrate your good points and accept your imperfections, loving you in spite of them. This person is encouraging and supportive. If there was nobody like this in your life, use your imagination to imagine what they would be like and create an ideal parent for yourself inside your mind's eye.
- Now imagine yourself in a beautiful natural setting for the child part of you and the ideal parent to meet and have a conversation. This could be on a park bench or walking on a beach.
- Have the child part of you who is carrying shame tell the parent part all about how they feel and why, whilst the adult

just listens. Allow the child part of you to express their emotions fully and without judgement. After the child part has expressed themselves, have the parent part speak lovingly to the child part, explaining that they have nothing to be ashamed of in being their natural true self. That being their authentic self is who they were meant to be in the world and is the only way to discover happiness and to offer their unique gifts to the world. Take your time with this and allow the child part of you to ask any questions they have and to express themselves fully. Then have the parent part remind the child of all of the unique and special things about them, also expressing love and acceptance of the child through kind words, or a big hug, or both.

- When the child feels ready to release the shame they've been carrying around this aspect of themselves, have them visualise the emotional energy of shame as a coloured mist and have this mist gather into one place in your body, before releasing it deep down into the earth via your grounding tree trunk.
- When all feelings of shame around this aspect are cleared, have the ideal parent gently hug the child part as they merge back within you.
- Repeat this exercise for all aspects of yourself on your list, and at any time when you experience shame around just being yourself.

Authentic Empowered Self Technique

Before using this technique do the grounding and awareness exercises at the beginning of Part 2 of the book.

- Find yourself a comfortable quiet pace where you know you're not going to be disturbed and either sit or lie down.
- Close your eyes and take a few deep relaxing breaths until your body begins to relax, allowing your mind to become focused.

- When you're feeling nice and relaxed, allow yourself to begin to picture your Authentic Empowered Self in your mind's eye. This is you at your best! Feeling confident, happy, at peace with who you are and enthusiastic about your future. Don't actively try too hard to picture yourself this way, just allow your mind and imagination to work for you. Ask your mind to show you what your Authentic Self would look like and allow that image to take form inside your mind. Don't question the image, just trust your mind and go with it.
- Now begin to notice things about the image of your Empowered Self. How are you dressed? How are you standing, or sitting? Notice your facial expression; do you look happy? Peaceful? Content? Notice the energy around your Empowered Self, how does that feel? Is it charged with positive feelings?
- As you begin to feel familiar with your Empowered Self, begin to gently drift into the image of yourself, so that you are inside your own body, looking out of your own eyes.
- Notice how it feels to be feeling truly authentic, and the natural empowerment that goes along with that. Do you feel confident and comfortable? If you do, that's great. If you're not feeling confident and comfortable, explore for a moment why that might be, and if there is anything you would like to adjust or add to the image of your Empowered Self to achieve feelings of confidence and comfort, do it now.
- Draw your awareness inside your body inside the centre of your head, looking out of your eyes and take a moment to allow yourself to experience feelings of self-acceptance, self-love, confidence and peace. Allow these feelings to flood your body from your head to your toes like a powerful elixir of positive energy flowing throughout your entire body and notice the easy and natural energy flow that comes along with integrated self-acceptance.
- Now take a moment to imagine three potentially challenging situations that could possibly arise in your life in the near future and play each of these scenarios out in detail in your

mind as you remain in your Empowered Self. Notice how you handle each situation, how you hold yourself and interact with other people. Notice your energy as you move through each situation and how you're feeling.

- Now, whilst still inside your Authentic Empowered Self, gently begin asking yourself, 'What's my purpose in life?' What do I really love doing?' 'What am I good at?' 'What am I here to do?' Patiently and gently ask these searching questions and allow the answers to emerge from your imagination. The answers may emerge in the form of words, pictures, symbols or feelings. Just as with all of the techniques in this book, the key is not to push, but to *allow* the answers to come to you. Relax and move out of your own way and the answers will arrive.
- When receiving answers, remain aware that nobody knows you or your capabilities better than you do. If your mind offers you answers that seem like too big a dream or ambition, don't close your mind and dismiss them out of fear or disbelief. Instead, keep your mind open so that you're able to run with the ideas and receive insights as to how to achieve them.
- When you feel that you have some idea of your purpose (it doesn't need to be a concrete idea), visualise yourself fulfilling your purpose as you remain inside your Empowered Self looking out of your own eyes. Again, notice how you look, walk, talk and interact with people as you go about living your life's purpose.
- Lastly, allow the experience of being in your Authentic Empowered Self to imprint your consciousness, feeling the energy of the experience powerfully filling your body from your head to the tips of your toes. You could give this energy a colour that you associate with being you at your best.
- Use this technique daily to keep you focused and on track in fulfilling your dreams and also as an aid to achieving a better experience of life on a daily basis.

Belief Alchemist Worksheets

Exercise 1: How your beliefs were created

Consider the beliefs you currently hold about yourself and the world and compare them to your family's view of you.

How my family view me	How I view myself	My world view (what I expect from the world)

Exercise 2: How your beliefs were created

Now consider what you have learned from using the Family of Origin technique, and re-enter your revised set of beliefs about yourself and the world in the boxes below.

How I view myself	My world view (what I expect from the world)

Exercise 3: A deeper look at your beliefs

Enter any beliefs and their effects in the table below.

Belief	Effect

Exercise 4: A deeper dive into your beliefs

Enter any conscious negative beliefs in the conscious beliefs column below.

After you have explored and reconsidered any conscious negative beliefs you have been carrying about yourself using the list of questions provided, enter your new, realistic beliefs in the column below under revised realistic conscious beliefs.

Negative/unrealistic conscious beliefs	Revised realistic conscious beliefs

Exercise 5: Self-consciousness

Begin to become aware of the way you speak to yourself and record the kinds of things you say to yourself on a regular basis. As your awareness of your self-talk grows, you will be amazed to discover how you have been speaking to yourself and the effect it has been having on your energy levels and your self-esteem.

Negative self-talk	Positive self-talk

Exercise 6: It's great to be different

Consider and list some of the important decisions you have made over the years, how you arrived at them, and how they worked out...

Decisions that worked out well and why	Decisions that did not work out so well, and why

Congratulations!

'You can only become truly self-confident when you accept, love and honour all that you are' ~ Maria J McMahon 😊

Congratulations! You have reached the end of the book and become your own *Belief Alchemist*! I hope that you have found this book helpful and inspiring, and that your beliefs about yourself and the world have transformed to the point that you are able to move forward in your life with much more confidence and optimism, knowing that you truly are the master of your own destiny and the creator of your own world.

Best wishes for a happy andsuccessful future,

Maria J McMahon.

About the Author

Maria J McMahon DipPCH, MNLP, TFT-Alg, SNLP, GQHP

Maria is an Intuitive Life Coach, Clinical Hypnotherapist, Energy Healer and Trauma Recovery Specialist, experienced in working with clients to heal and clear any blocks that stand between them and manifesting a life they love.

Being born intuitive and sensitive to energy sparked in Maria a natural interest in metaphysics, especially in how it relates to the human psyche. This interest led her to study Neuro-linguistic programming with Dr Richard Bandler, after which she trained as a Clinical Hypnotherapist and Life Coach. Later, she also trained as a Thought Field Therapist and a Psychometric Assessor.

Maria's training in combination with her work with clients who had experienced challenging childhoods, led her to discover that our minds are very much programmed during childhood, and that our experiences (especially traumatic ones) have the potential to wire into our minds limiting beliefs that hide away in our subconscious, keeping us from our natural ability to manifest a life we love.

Through working with her own subconscious mind and teaching her clients how to do the same, Maria found that it is entirely possible to hack into the subconscious and to clear out any limiting beliefs hiding away there. This allows us to reprogram our minds with beliefs that are in alignment with the truth of who we are, and with the manifestation of our dreams.

Maria wrote Belief Alchemist as a step -by -step guide for this process, to help as many people as possible to rediscover the creative power of the human mind, and to join others around the globe in manifesting a better world.

If you would like to work with Maria to clear any blocks that are keeping you from manifesting a life you love, one -to -one coaching is available at: www.mariajmcmahon.com

Testimonials from People Who Have Used the Belief Alchemist Techniques

'I walked into Maria's room a mess, a broken individual. Life had provided so much for me, but I was unable to enjoy it, paralysed by insecurities, low self-esteem, avoidance strategies and plagued by self-sabotage. I was unable to realise any potential because I carried around some unconscious guilt that I didn't deserve happiness or rather I just wasn't used to normal feelings of balance, acceptance and positive self-esteem. Maria transformed my life and put me in a place where I can not only enjoy my life, but am happy to explore and embrace the opportunities that are open to me. I had always considered myself to be perceptive and intuitive capable of a spiritual existence. Maria made me work, she had at her disposal tool techniques that surprised me, shook me to the core, and awakened me to my true self.' ~ Simon.

'I came to see Maria at a very difficult time in my life. All of my three long term relationships had ended badly. I blamed myself for these failures and had a set of issues I'd brought from childhood experiences into these relationships. I felt something had to change, I had no sense of who I was or where I was going in my life. I'm quite a spiritual person, my view of life doesn't exactly fit with mainstream ideas. I was nervous about seeing a therapist because I struggle with mainstream psychology, it doesn't work for me. I find it somehow scripted and condescending. My fears however were put to rest in my first therapy session with Maria. Maria is instantly likeable, very friendly and authentic. Maria exudes confidence in what she does. She genuinely cares, has a great sense of humour and instantly put me at ease. I was in a bad place when I first saw Maria and now when I look at my life it's completely different. It's like I'm a different person, I'm more confident in myself and my own abilities. Before I was largely dependent on other people and now I stand very much on my own with great confidence that I'm moving in the right direction. With Maria's positive attitude, professionalism and my own hard work and determination we worked together to change my life completely. I couldn't thank Maria enough for what she has done for me.' ~ Martin.

'I have known Maria J McMahon in a professional capacity for 3 years and would highly recommend her as an extremely competent Therapist and Practitioner. Her attention to detail and aptitude to get to the heart of the matter is an incredible catalyst for authentic self-development.' ~ Jane.

Printed in Great Britain
by Amazon

87196083R00078